1988

Helping Troubled Families:

A Social Work Perspective

George Thorman

ALDINE PUBLISHING COMPANY
NEW YORK

ALDINE

First published 1982
Aldine Publishing Company
200 Saw Mill River Road
Hawthorne, New York 10532

ISBN 0-202-26091-7 cloth; 0-202-26092-5 paper

Library of Congress Catalog Number 81-67975

Printed in the United States of America

10   9   8   7   6   5   4   3   2   1

With much appreciation for
   —*the family that loved me as a child*
   —*the family that loves me as a husband
     and father*
   —*the families that turned to me for help
     and accepted me as a friend.*

These are some of the things that our fourth grade class thought were important family problems. Here is a list of the problems we discussed. One of the problems is divorce. Divorce is hard on the child for many reasons. They have to learn to cope with new situations and sometimes they have to choose which parent to live with. That's hard. Another thing that is hard is hunger. Many children in the U.S. go through many days without food. Parents who lose their jobs don't have enough money to pay for the proper foods. Loneliness is also hard for children. Some children are alone for many hours a day. Some children's parents are in jail or prison. This can be a serious problem. Children must often learn to accept the illness or death of a parent. We hope you will discuss these problems at your meeting and find some ways to help children.

—*Letter to the White House Conference on the Family from a fourth grade class.*

Table of Contents

Preface

1. *Introduction* *1*

2. *Perspectives on the Family* *7*
The Family Life Cycle; The Social Environment; Basic Family Processes; Healthy Families; Troubled Families; Assessing Family Systems.

3. *Approaches to Helping* *41*
Behavioral Social Work; Crisis Intervention; Family Therapy; Group Therapy; Multiple Family Therapy; Network Intervention.

4. *Solving Family Problems* *65*
Solving Marital Problems; Helping Separated Persons; Changing Parent-Child Relationships; Improving Individual Adjustment; Changing Environmental Conditions; Family Advocacy.

5. *Helping Disorganized Families* *101*
An Overview; The Helping Process; Problem-Solving Approaches; Task Planning; Shared Problem-Solving Tasks; Problem-Solving and Communication; Effectiveness of Problem-Solving.

6. *Working with Abusive Families* *131*
Violence Begets Violence; Social Stress and Child Abuse; Dysfunctions in Abusive Families; Approach to Helping; Using Community Resources; Protective Services; Preventive Measures.

7. *Acquiring Skills* *155*
Behavioral Social Work Training; Training in Network Intervention; Training in Family Therapy; Teaching Aids; Training Through Supervision; Training Centers.

8. *Applying Theories Relevant to Practice* *173*
Systems Theory; Role Theory; Communication Theory; Social Learning Theory; Combining and Integrating.

Preface

This book is an introduction to contemporary methods and techniques employed by social workers to help troubled families cope with a wide range of problems. Although some of the theories and concepts that developed in family therapy have been incorporated in the text, this is not a book about family therapy. The intent is to set forth the basic principles of social work practice with families and to provide a clear, concise source of information that can be used by social workers in their day-by-day practice. The book is also designed to serve as a text for undergraduate and graduate courses in schools of social work.

The introductory chapter outlines the role that the family plays in the development of the person and the basic functions it performs: providing security for its members, offering opportunities for personal growth, helping family members achieve self-identity and socializing the young into adult roles. Chapter Two provides a perspective on the family that is the basis for social work intervention. The life cycle of the family is outlined and the processes of family interaction are described. This chapter also points out the factors that distinguish between healthy families and dysfunctional families and indicates the major areas in which problems occur.

Chapter Three describes five major methods of working with families: behavior modification, crisis intervention, family therapy, group therapy and social network intervention. These particular models have been chosen because they are especially useful in working with the majority of clients who come to the attention of social workers. Chapter Four proceeds to give detailed attention to the techniques involved in helping families through the use of the problem-solving process in working with marital problems, parent-child relationship problems and problems of individual adjustment. The importance of solving problems related to adverse environmental conditions is emphasized and the role of the social worker as family advocate is described as an effective form of intervention.

Chapter Five introduces the reader to the nature of disorganized, multiproblem families and the steps involved in working with "hard-to-reach" families. The use of specific techniques in intervention is also described, with special attention given to the role that the social worker plays in helping these families attain a higher and more adequate level of social functioning. The importance of establishing a trusting relationship and providing concrete services to meet the family's needs is emphasized.

Chapter Six focuses on abusive families, the dynamics of interaction that characterizes these family systems and the factors that produce aggression and physical violence against children. Attention is given to the methods that can be used to make the family a safe environment for the child by providing auxiliary social services, lay therapists, crisis centers and foster care. Chapter Seven indicates how social workers can prepare for family social work and outlines the skills needed to become a competent family casework practitioner. Chapter Eight summarizes the different approaches towards dealing with troubled families, and discusses the varying goals and the differing roles of the social worker within each theory. Case studies have been used extensively to illustrate the application of the social work process in working with troubled families.

Much of what I have written has grown out of my experience as a family social work practitioner, researcher and educator. As a public assistance worker I came face to face with the pervasive poverty that enveloped families living in the inner city of a midwestern metropolitan area. I saw young mothers trying desperately to make ends meet on the meager allowance granted to them to support their children. I saw their children going to school hungry and going to bed hungry. These were the "multiproblem families" — a euphemism for those who had to cope with too many problems despite too few resources.

After completing my graduate education, I joined the staff of a family service agency and began to recognize that middle class families had problems of a somewhat different order. I counseled couples trying to revitalize their relationships or striving to overcome the serious interpersonal conflicts that destroy marriages. I saw parents confused and dismayed by the behavior of their teenage children, who wondered, "Where did we go wrong?" I helped families cope with grave and disrupting crisis situations: the hospitalization of a family member, the onslaught of a mental illness, the fear of an impending death.

As researcher and educator, I began to study seriously the structure and dynamics of family living to discover what makes it possible for the family to survive and what those in the helping profession can do to make that survival less difficult. I owe much of what I have learned to the families who turned to me in time of trouble. I hope that what they taught me will be useful to others engaged in the human enterprise of helping troubled families.

Helping Troubled Families:

A Social Work Perspective

ONE

Introduction

*The emotional give and take
of family relationships is the
crucial center of forces that
make or break mental health.*
—Nathan Ackerman

The family has an enduring impact on the development
of the person. The family shapes the child's personality, attitudes,
behavior and beliefs. Although a person may change in some respects
during his or her lifetime, the influence of the family in the development of personality cannot be completely undone. Because the family plays such an important role in this development, social workers
and other helping professionals have a continuing concern about the
family and the welfare of its members. The current interest in family
therapy as an effective method for helping troubled families to resolve
problems and to function more adequately is an outgrowth of this
longstanding professional interest and concern.

Family Functions
The family carries out several important functions. It provides a
safe and secure environment for the young, teaches skills essential
to the performance of adult tasks, and offers opportunities for the

personal growth and emotional development of its members.

Providing security. All families are called upon to provide a safe, secure environment for the young. Indeed, the very survival of children depends on the parents' ability to meet the child's basic physical needs: food, clothing, shelter, and health care. However, some families are not able to provide adequately for their children. And these the poor families make up a shockingly high proportion of the population. More than a quarter of all American children live in families that subsist on one half the median income for all U.S. families. More than sixty percent of the children in the United States live in female-headed households. They constitute a large percentage of the families that fall below the poverty line. For children under six years of age, the percentage of those living in poverty rises to seventy-five percent in single, female-headed families. Almost six out of ten black children grow up with less than the minimum income needed to provide adequate food, clothing and shelter. In 1974, more than seventeen million children were living in families trying to survive on less than half the median income in the United States. As the Carnegie Council on Children points out, the damage done to children who live in poverty is painfully distressing.

"The children whose parents lack the security of a regular job are usually the same children who are undernourished and who live in inadequate housing," says the Council. "Poor prenatal care and more frequent infant deaths are closely connected with low income. ...Inadequate prenatal care for pregnant women increases the chances that children will be born premature, disabled, sickly or dead" (Keniston, 1977, p. 32).

Families beset by the grim reality of poverty usually face a wide range of serious problems, in addition to poor health. Mental health and emotional well-being are grossly impaired; delinquency and crime become the accepted ways of dealing with the frustration of living on the edge of starvation and death. Family relationships often become severely strained under the pressure of poverty, the stress that comes with inadequate income, poor housing, and not enough food to nourish and sustain life. Such pressures may eventually end in desertion, divorce, hospitalization, or imprisonment.

These families have been labeled "multiproblem families"; they face the most serious problems with the least resources. They are the victims of a society that directs only a minimal amount of its economic resources to improve the quality of their lives. Because of the persistence of poverty, "One child in every four in America is being actively harmed by a stacked deck created by the failings of our society," says the Carnegie Council report. Social workers have been concerned about the plight of these families for many decades. Chapter Five focuses on what can be done to help them cope with the stress of living in poverty.

Giving protection. Protection from danger is as vital to the survival of the young as the provision of material needs. The family is regarded as the one place where the person is safe. It is the haven that shelters from the hazards of the outside world. In times of crisis and acute stress, family members seek out the protection of the home to recuperate from personal injuries, psychological hurts, or great emotional upheavals. The family is supposed to be available at all times to provide the necessary protection for both children and adults.

By far the majority of families meet this test in time of trouble; but in some cases, the family is a dangerous place to live. In these violent families marital conflict explodes in dangerous attacks against women and children, parents abuse children, and husbands batter their wives. The art of communication and negotiation of conflicts is not found in such families. Physical force is the only method used to cope with family problems, and violence becomes a commonplace experience in the family's day-to-day life.

The prevalance of family violence and the harm that it inflicts on its victims is a matter of serious concern among lay and professional groups. Studies indicate that some form of violence will take place in one out of six families each year. Women, as well as children, are badly damaged, both physically and emotionally. It is astonishing to record that one half of all homicides take place in the family environment. Police report that a major portion of the calls to which they respond involve violence or threats of violence between husband and wife.

Because society has entrusted social agencies with the responsibility to protect children from neglect and abuse, family violence is a matter of grave concern to the social work profession. Social workers have begun to study the underlying causes of family violence and to develop new approaches to the prevention of child abuse and wifebeating. Chapter Six will focus on the application of family social work as one of the methods employed in the treatment and prevention of family violence.

Socialization of the person. The family is largely responsible for socialization, developing basic concepts of right and wrong and encouraging acceptable social behavior. Failure to develop a conscience sufficiently strong to control behavior can usually be traced to faulty childhood training. Children who grow up in families where there is an absence of training and no limits are placed on behavior fail to develop the internal controls needed to curb dangerous aggressive acts. Persons who have grown up in abusive, violent families and have been subjected to harsh punishment as children often become violent, aggressive, hostile adults who in turn abuse their wives and children or become involved in assault and homicide. These are the psychopaths who feel no obligation to cooperate with others or to conform to the rules that govern the behavior of law-abiding people.

The family is also responsible for preparing the young to carry out adult roles, especially family roles such as husband and wife, mother and father. Children look to their parents for providing the models to follow when they form their own families. Children observe their parents interacting and relating to each other. These observations have a strong influence on the nature and quality of the relationships they establish with their future marriage partners, or how they will resolve problems in interpersonal relations and how they will cope with the outside world. Moreover, the development of a capacity for intimacy takes place within the family. Through the process of relating to other family members, the person gradually becomes aware of the meaning of intimacy, learns how such relationships are formed and maintained. If the individual has had few opportunities to experience feelings of closeness and intimacy within his/her own family as s/he grew up, s/he may have serious difficulty forming intimate ties as an adult. The inability to form and maintain such ties will often result in repeated failures in marriage or a series of love relationships that end in frustration and disappointment.

Encouraging personal growth. The maturation of the person, the development of a sense of identity and the ability to act responsibly are largely products of experience within the family from birth through adolescence and even into adult life. The family helps the young develop a sense of uniqueness by recognizing their special talents, particular personality traits, and distinct ways of behaving and thinking. By so doing, the family encourages the child to develop a strong feeling of self-identity and individuality. Persons uncertain or confused about their values, roles, strengths or abilities experience what Erikson (1950) refers to as an "identity crisis." While each individual is called upon to resolve this crisis through his/her own efforts, the family either facilitates this effort to achieve a secure sense of identity or inhibits efforts to achieve individuality.

Evidence that some families are so constituted that they produce serious personality problems and mental disorders is beginning to come to light. Faulty patterns of communication and dysfunctional forms of interpersonal relationships within the family appear to be related to the emergence of neurotic or psychotic symptoms in one of the family members. Chapter Two explores how the family system impacts on the mental health of its members and the extent to which it affects their emotional state.

Dr. Nathan Ackerman, one of the pioneers in family therapy, describes the importance of the family in this eloquent passage:

> The purpose and functions of family life are multiple. They have to do with security and survival, sexual union and fulfillment, the care of the young and the aged, the cultivation of a bond of affection and identity, and training for the tasks of social participation. Beyond the prime task of protecting the biological integrity and the growth potential of the off-spring, the main on-going function of the family group is to support the continued socialization and humanization of its members, children and adults alike. When family life fails, the inevitable consequence is a tendency toward dehumanization of human behavior (Ackerman, 1961, p. 53).

Because the family plays such an important role in the development of the person, social workers have turned their attention to finding effective programs for the treatment and prevention of family disorganization. Intervention aimed at correcting faulty functioning can and must be undertaken to help families cope with problems in new and more effective ways. That is the subject of this book.

References

Ackerman, N. (Ed.). *Exploring the base for family therapy*. New York: Family Service Association of America, 1961.

Erikson, E. *Childhood and society*. New York: W. W. Norton, 1950.

Keniston, K. & Carnegie Council on Children. *All our children: The American family under pressure*. New York: Harcourt Brace Jovanovich, 1977.

TWO

Perspectives on the Family

Families vary in their ability to protect the young and help them grow into mature, responsible adults free of psychiatric symptoms. Families also differ greatly in the ability to cope with stress. Some have enough personal and material resources to deal with family and personal problems. They can survive a crisis without a permanent disruption of the family system. Other families are very vulnerable to stress and fall apart in times of crisis because they are ill prepared to cope with problems. Why they sometimes falter in carrying out their functions and responsibilities is related to these basic factors: (1) their relative ability to accommodate to the progressive stages of the family life cycle; (2) the nature of the basic processes of family interaction that maintain the current family system; and (3) the quality of the social environment that surrounds the family.

An effective approach in helping troubled families is based upon a careful evaluation of these three basic aspects of family functioning. Social work practitioners therefore inquire into all these facets of the life of the families who seek their help before they begin to embark upon solving the problems that their clients present. Therefore, the first step in the helping process consists of making a sound assessment of the family as a basis for social intervention.

Family Life Cycle

A useful way to think about the family system is to study how it develops and changes during the course of its lifetime. Every family goes through certain developmental stages and each stage requires the family members to make adjustments to the changes involved in moving from one stage to the next. A recently married couple must be able to reconcile their different expectations of one another and what they expect from marriage. Middle-age parents must be able to cope with problems common to rearing adolescent children trying to find their own self-identity and gain freedom from parental authority. The parents themselves are called upon to work through their own "midlife crisis" while attempting to adjust to changes in their relationships with their children. The physical, economic and emotional changes that accompany the aging process become sources of anxiety, especially in the postretirement period when parents become more dependent on other family members.

The ability of the family to pass from one stage of the life cycle to the next is an important consideration in putting clients' problems within the perspective of a developmental framework. In some cases, the family has serious difficulty making the transition from one stage to the next, and the family system is disrupted by the failure to fulfill essential tasks at a specific point in the life cycle. Family members may experience considerable emotional distress and develop psychiatric symptoms when the family's normal development is disrupted by some event outside its control, such as divorce, separation or an important loss. Other events, such as the arrival of a new child or a young adult leaving the family, have an impact on family relationships at critical points. Each of the stages of family life cycle suggests that family problems can often be traced to the difficulties and problems associated with a specific period of development.

During the early marriage period, the couple must complete two important tasks. The first is to complete the separation from their parents and strengthen the bonds between themselves in starting their own family. Difficulty in accomplishing this task ensues if either partner has not developed his own self-identity and matured into an autonomous and responsible adult. The capacity to form a satisfactory relationship of intimacy with the marital partner is based upon the ability of both husband and wife to transfer feelings of affection from their parents to their spouses. In some cases, this task is not accomplished easily or rapidly. If the partners grew up in families that encouraged the development of autonomy and independence, the task is not insurmountable and the marital relationship is gradually strengthened within the first year or two.

During the early phase of marriage, the couple must also complete a second important task, namely to establish the basic rules of their relationship as husband and wife. During their courtship, some couples will already have made some progress in this direction and have clarified what they expect after marriage, but in any case the couple needs to develop mutual understanding. They will need to decide how power will be used, who makes decisions about what, and how to resolve differences in opinion. Rules about relationships evolve gradually in such matters as how close or how distant the partners want to remain from one another, which feelings are to be expressed openly and which kept private. The couple must also begin to develop negotiating and communicating skills in order to find ways of trading off, learning to find out what each is willing to give up in exchange for something from the partner. During this period the couple also develops fairly stable and satisfactory patterns in regard to sex, relationships with in-laws, involvement with friends and the responsibility for money management and household duties.

If the couple has been reasonably successful in completing these tasks during the early part of marriage, they will be ready to move into the next stage in the family life cycle, becoming parents. The birth of the first child is an important point in the family life cycle, requiring that both partners take on new roles as parents in addition to continuing to perform their roles of husband and wife. The infant child makes many demands on the mother for physical care: feeding, changing diapers, and attending to the baby occupy much of her time. The young mother will be inexperienced in her new role, often uncertain as to how well she is living up to the additional responsibilities of caring for a helpless infant.

Understanding and assistance from the husband can make the task of mothering less difficult. During this period the couple must come to some agreement as to how much responsibility the father will take in child-rearing. If the mother excludes the father from the care of the children, or if the father excludes himself voluntarily, the experience of parenting will not be fully shared. Both parents can achieve a great deal of satisfaction from the infant and from parenting. If they do not share in this experience, the relationship between them may be weakened. In many families the mother takes on the full role of care-taker and the father takes on the role of earning a living and being the provider. For some families, this distinct separation of parental roles is preferred, but in others the marital partners find an advantage in sharing roles. Mothers may choose to re-enter the job market as the children grow older and become less dependent on parental care and supervision. The husband's cooperation in enabling the mother to work outside the home is paramount if the family is to remain stable and adjust to the change in family roles.

The family faces another important problem during the first parenting stage; they must be able to maintain a satisfactory relationship as marriage partners while adjusting to their role as parents. There is always the possibility that the wife may become so involved in mothering that she fails to give adequate attention to her husband's needs for support, affection, and sexual gratification. During this time alignments between the children and the mother may cause the father to feel shut out of the family circle. Or he may turn to another woman for the love and attention that he does not receive from his wife. Or the wife may find her husband so preoccupied with the need to succeed as breadwinner that he has little energy to give to his role as husband and father. A growing sense of disappointment may push her into asking for a divorce or cause her to find refuge in alcohol. During the first parenting period the relationship between the parents will deepen or conflicts between them will increase. The couple may have tried to hide their increasing resentment from one another and from the children. However, eventually these undercover conflicts will break into the open and threaten the solidarity of the family. If the parents' relationship has continued to grow and deepen, they will have developed an understanding of one another, developed satisfactory rules for their relationship, and be highly supportive of one another.

After the children have left the family and settled into lives of their own, the parents often experience new happiness in their relationship as husband and wife. Having survived all the troubles that beset them during the parenting period, they now feel much closer and develop a more satisfying relationship than at any other point in their marriage. It is quite possible that the marriage was in a quiescent state during child-rearing. The parents had little time to give to the marital relationship because of their children's demands. With the children grown and the responsibilities lifted, they can devote their time and energy to their marriage.

A study of the problems that clients bring to family service agencies indicates a close relationship between stages in the family life cycle and the type of problem families seek help with. In the period before the children are born, marital problems are the chief focus for requests for service. Personality problems come second, indicating that couples who have difficulty accommodating to the marital relation also have personality problems requiring attention. Family and home management problems rank third in frequency during the early part of the marriage, an indication of the stress involved in establishing a home and determining the role functions of husband and wife.

As the family circle expands with the arrival of new children, a variety of problems begins to come to the fore. The family experiences problems in child-related areas and these take on more importance. By the time the oldest child enters school, the demand for service for children's problems surpass marital and adult personality problems. By the time that children reach adolescence, they make up ninety percent of all requests regarding problems in family relationships. Marital problems remain at a plateau until the children leave home, at which point there is a sharp decline in requests for help in solving marital problems.

At the beginning of the empty nest-period, with the onset of the aging process, health and caretaking problems begin to be the major areas of concern for the family. With the coming of the retirement years, relationship problems decline and are replaced by an ever increasing load of practical problems. As the old age approaches, forty percent of the problems for which the family seeks help involve health, caretaking and home management, and it is at this point that the capacity to cope with these problems begins to diminish (Beck, 1973).

Most middle-class American families generally go through the life cycle in a fixed pattern; families form when people marry, separate from their parents, learn to accommodate to each other as marital partners and assume the role of parents with the arrival of their first child. Each addition to the family not only increases its size, but reorganizes the family structure, its living pattern and its life style in some important respects. As families mature, new parent/child relationships are established and the relationship between the mother and the father may also change in the process. The family system must accommodate itself to this expansion phase. It must also accommodate itself to the contraction stage when the family size shrinks as the older children leave to form their own families. Each stage in the family life cycle is accompanied by special problems that relate to this process of accommodation, and each family must find a suitable and effective way to resolve these problems so that the family unit and individual family members can move on to the next stage of growth and personal development.

The Social Environment

Families do not live in a vacuum. They are surrounded by a complex social, economic and cultural environment that has a profound impact on the family as a whole and on the lives of its members. All families must be able to cope with this social environment in order to survive. The social environment is benign to some families and destructive to others. Therefore, a perspective on family systems includes a consideration of important forces in the family's social and cultural environment, including: (1) the immediate neighborhood in which the family lives; (2) the community that surrounds the family; (3) the larger social system and the position that the family occupies in the social structure.

Neighborhoods. Families are often identified by the neighborhoods in which they live. Some neighborhoods are dangerous. They are beset by excessive and violent crimes. The families who live in such unsafe neighborhoods are the victims of murder, rape, assault and other forms of violence. Living in such conditions creates major psychological as well as practical problems for the inhabitants. Mothers are afraid that their children will be harmed; they therefore try to restrict play activities to safe areas. Adults are on guard at all times for possible attacks. A general aura of fear grips the family and hangs like a dark cloud over people unable to move to less dangerous neighborhoods.

Some neighborhoods are characterized by substandard rundown housing, poorly lighted streets, and vacant buildings. These are the urban slums and the barrios where the poor live in isolated neighborhoods separated from the rest of society. The small houses in these areas are occupied by large families with eight or ten persons sharing a three-room house or a two-room apartment. The effect of living in such overcrowded housing conditions is seen in the rapid spread of contagious disease, dehumanization and loss of self-esteem.

The need for a supportive network of friendly neighbors goes unmet in many of these neighborhoods, but this is not always the case. In many barrios, there is a concern for the welfare of one's neighbors. In times of adversity or crisis, the family can call upon the help of those living nearby. In many cases, the assistance of this social network is one of the few positive resources on which the family can rely in times of adversity.

Communities. In large urban centers, the community is usually bounded by natural barriers such as a river or by artificial barriers such as a railroad or busy freeway. The type community the family lives in also has an impact on the family. Some communities provide ample, high-quality facilities for residents while other communities do not meet the basic requirements for decent family living.

Among the resources provided by the community are the schools to which the families send their children. The quality of education that the children receive depends on how adequately the community provides funds for teachers' salaries, for the construction and maintenance of the buildings, and back-up materials such as books, visual aids, and laboratory equipment. In communities occupied by poor families, the quality of education leaves much to be desired. The teachers are usually less qualified and less enthusiastic about their teaching enterprise than those who teach in affluent, well financed school districts. The physical plant in the "poorer sections of town" are the oldest and most run-down buildings in the school system. The attitudes of teachers and school administrators toward students in these communities is detrimental to learning and high achievement. Little wonder that students drop out of the educational system and are poorly suited to find employment and gain financial security.

Health and sanitation services are often woefully inadequate in the communities the troubled families we will concentrate on inhabit. Building codes are violated. Housing inspection and enforcement of standards set by law are either ignored or by-passed by landlords who have no interest in the condition of the houses they rent to these families. Rats and vermin run rampant and uncontrolled in the tenement areas of these communities. Fires break out and endanger the lives of the elderly and the children who cannot escape the smoke and flames. Broken plumbing fixtures go unrepaired and become sources of disease and infection for infants and children. Epidemics of contagious disease spread rapidly in these communities because of the lack of good sanitation.

Police protection is regarded as essential to all families. Yet many families living in housing projects report that police do not promptly respond to their calls for protection. Sometimes they do not respond at all. Minority groups report that in their communities, the police are oppressors rather than protectors of the citizens who live there. Reports and accusations of police abuse of minorities are common in almost every urban area, causing some residents to take a very cynical attitude toward equal justice and protection under the law.

Troubled families are often single-parent families, headed either by a mother dependent on a meager public assistance grant or with an unskilled low-paying job. These families need adequate facilities for the care of pre-school children while the mother works. Yet many communities, *most* communities, in which these families live pro-

vide no free day-care nursery facilities for the children of working
mothers. Under those conditions, the opportunity for mothers of
these families to become self-supporting are very remote and the
repeated admonition to "get off the welfare rolls" is highly ineffective and even blatantly insulting.

Social system and social structure. The quality of family life, the
ability of families to survive, depends in large measure on their
position in the social structure. Families in a favorable, high-status
or upper-class position have a distinct advantage over those in the
lowest socio-economic strata of the social order. Life opportunities
are much more abundant to rich and middle-class families. Children
in low-income families have less chance to enter higher education
than children in upper-class families. Education opens the way for
better jobs and higher income. Without the credentials of better
education, the children in lower-class families are denied the opportunity to move up into better paying, more personally satisfying jobs.

The impact of poverty on the lives of families is serious and multi-
faceted. Those in the lowest socio-eonomic strata are far more likely
to have serious health problems and chronic disabilities. The life
span of the adults in these families is shorter by nine or ten years
than the average longevity of the general population. More mothers
die in childbirth and more children born to them die before the end
of the first year of life. Lack of proper food or enough food causes
malnutrition in the mother and the child. Malnutrition in the child
leads to learning disabilities, poor health and a limited amount of
energy available to achieve. Children in these families fall behind
other pupils, face the constant threat of failure, and drop out before
completing high school.

The effect of poverty on the mental health of family members has
been pointed out by the Hollingshead and Redlick study of an urban
community (Hollingshead, 1958). Serious mental illness that takes
the form of psychosis is found disproportionately frequently among
persons in the lowest socio-economic class. And these are the types
of psychosis that are the most disabling and that require hospitalization. Persons in lower-class groups usually receive little intensive
psychiatric treatment; their stay in a state hospital is longer than those
patients who fall into the middle- and upper-classes of society.

Perhaps the most devastating psychological effect of poverty and
social inequality is the pervasive feeling of hopelessness and alienation found in many low-income, low-status families. Lack of opportunity brings on a sense of hopelessness about the future and despair

about changing conditions for the betterment of oneself and one's family. The sense of powerlessness in the face of overwhelming social and environmental conditions leads to a feeling of alienation from the mainstream of society. Isolation and alienation add to the frustration and contribute to the low self-esteem so frequently found in these families.

Social workers have a long tradition of concern for those family and individual victims of social and economic inequalities. In working with troubled families, social workers themselves will often experience many of the same frustrations and feelings of hopelessness as their clients. In working with these troubled families, one becomes aware of the crying need for a more enlightened and humane social policy that will improve the life of many families with severely restricted opportunities.

The unequal impact of the social environment on families is an important consideration in assessing troubled families. Among the clients who requested service from family service agencies, those in the lowest socio-economic level reported six times as many environmental problems per family as clients in the upper socio-economic strata. For the nonwhite clients, the impact of the social environment is particularly stressful. For the nonwhite group, the average number of problems reported was almost triple the number reported by the total white group of clients, according to a survey conducted by the Family Service Association of America (Beck, 1973). In short, poor families and minority families feel the impact of adverse environmental factors much more frequently than middle-class, white families.

Nonwhite and poor families also reported a high number of family relationship and personal adjustment problems in addition to the environmental problems they were facing. The survey indicates that families in the lower economic strata must bear a very heavy load of both family and environmental problems. At the same time, they have the least material and personal resources to cope with problems. The toll taken on these families in terms of personal suffering is tremendous, making it incumbent on the social workers who serve them to take the lead in advocating the elimination and correction of the environmental conditions that have a serious adverse impact on the family. The role of social workers in changing environmental conditions by acting as advocates for troubled families is described in Chapter Four.

Basic Family Processes

The family system is maintained by certain basic processes through which family members interact with one another in predictable patterns. Family members learn to expect certain kinds of behavior and responses from other family members. These interaction patterns form a network that holds the family together during its lifetime. The basic processes which underlie family interaction networks include the following: (1) adapting to social roles within the family structure; (2) establishing and maintaining relationships among family members; (3) developing pathways of communication to transmit and receive messages; and (4) creating ways of coping with conflict among family members.

Adaptation to social roles. The family is brought into being when two adults come into a relationship in which each must accept responsibility for performing certain social roles. The male partner as husband is expected to perform those tasks which society defines as appropriate to husbands. The female partner is expected to perform certain functions in her role as wife. The culture provides a set of guidelines that help the partners assume their social roles within the family systems. Custom and tradition prescribe that a husband will assume certain responsibilities and that a wife will in turn carry out responsibilities in accord with her position in the institution of marriage. In addition, the legal code incorporates these definitions of roles. A body of law generally reflects the customs and ideas about marital roles and responsibilities.

However, each couple finds it necessary to develop its own conception of the role definitions that they can accept and fulfill. Each partner brings to the marriage his or her ideas of what is expected of a wife or husband. These expectations are based upon cultural norms, but the family of origin also shapes each partner's view as to social roles. In the family of origin models of husband and wife are laid down in early childhood. The early imprint of socialization into roles is carried over into adult life and into the marital system when the new family is formed. If there is wide divergence in the models laid down in the families of origin, the problems of adjusting to social roles become more difficult than if the early imprints are quite similar. Social scientists have found that a person who marries a partner who comes from the same social class and shares the same cultural values and norms is likely to work out a more harmonious relationship than persons whose partners' family background, social class, and culture or ethnic values are dissimilar from their own.

Various examples of conflicting expectations in social roles illustrate the manner in which they become a source of confusion and difficulty between the partners. If the wife comes from a background in which the woman's role was rigidly defined as caretaker of husband and children, she will meet the needs and expectations of a partner who also accepts this definition of the wife's social role. On the other hand, if the wife comes from a family background in which high value is placed on success in a career and little importance is attached to nurturing, this same husband may find it difficult to accept that set of values. The wife's conception of her role and the husband's conception differ. Where there are conflicting expectations as to social roles, the couple usually can be helped to resolve these conflicts and make the necessary adjustments for the marriage to survive.

Since roles change at critical points in family life, the process of adjusting to social roles continues throughout the marriage. For example, with the birth of the first child, partners must take on new social roles — as parents. The couple is required to make the necessary new adjustments involved in becoming a father and a mother. Common sense has generally set down a maxim that the couple should not plan to have children unless they have first worked out a satisfactory adjustment to their roles as husband and wife. Social scientists have pointed out that the transition from one role to another during the life cycle makes many demands on the capacity of people to move from a familiar role to an unfamiliar one. To make the transition from being single to being married and from being married to becoming a parent is not accomplished without some psychological discomfort and anxiety. These periods of transition may present a crisis for the family and become a threat to its survival. References to the ''empty-nest syndrome'' indicate that the loss of the important role of parent when the children leave home and become increasingly independent is a significant factor in causing depressive states in mothers or causing the marital partners to re-examine their relationship as husband and wife.

The adjustment to social roles also requires a capacity to function as an adult if generational boundaries are to be maintained. A woman psychologically ill prepared to assume the role of mother will have difficulty fulfilling the task of nurturing a young child. The man who has difficulty establishing intimate ties with women will have great difficulty in providing satisfaction for his wife's emotional and sexual needs. Therefore, an inquiry into the capacity of the marital partners to function in their social roles becomes an important part of the study of the family system. If one or both adults lack the capacity to give what is required in their social roles, the family system is endangered.

Establishing and maintaining relationships. The existence of the
family depends upon the ability of family members to relate to one
another in ways which provide an adequate degree of autonomy
for each family member while at the same time not seriously
threatening or impairing the unity of the family. During the early
stages of marriage, the partners begin to develop patterns for their
relationship. They attempt to determine mutually acceptable amounts
of autonomy, independence, and freedom. For example, the wife is
free to manage the family income as long as she does not exceed an
agreed-upon amount. The husband is free to invite guests as long as
he gives the wife advance notice. In most families, these governing
rules are made on an *ad hoc* basis as the occasion demands. Eventually, they become understood to be mutually agreeable unless one or
the other partner raises the issue and a new rule is agreed upon.

In certain areas, rules about relationships are not clearly spelled
out. In the sexual area the couple may relate to one another on the
basis of rules which remain unspoken. For example, the husband is
always the partner who initiates sexual advance although there has
been no verbal agreement that this must always be the case. In other
areas, the wife may always "inform" her husband of her plans for
the day although not required to do so. Eventually, a series of such
unspoken rules become the working basis upon which the couple
proceed to relate to one another until some violation of the "unspoken
rule" calls the matter into question. For example, if the wife fails to
"inform" the husband, a sense of insecurity on his part may affect
the relationship. The husband becomes anxious and begins to question the wife about her daily activities. The wife may then begin to
question the right of the husband to intrude in an area which she
regards as private and the whole question of what is to be their
relationship is opened up for negotiation.

As in the matter of social roles, the relationship between family
members is in a state of flux due to changes in the life cycle of the
family. During the early stages of marriage, the couple may find that
they are content "to do everything together." Gradually, this close
symbiotic tie is no longer comfortable, and the partners evolve a
different relationship which permits more autonomy in the marriage
and gives more space to each partner. Or a marriage that began with
a relationship in which the wife was always submissive to the husband takes on a different character when the wife requests a change
to an egalitarian relationship. If the husband is unable to accept this
change, a struggle ensues, and the couple must redetermine the kind
of relationship that they are willing to maintain.

Relationships between parents and children are also subject to change during the family life cycle. As children reach an age when more independence and self-direction is demanded, the parents may become threatened by a change in the ties which have been established between themselves and their children at an earlier stage. Therefore, the family system must make allowances for new adaptations. Satisfactory and functional relationships do not remain so for all time. The ability of the family system to recognize the need for changing relationships in response to changed conditions and the capacity of the family to accommodate to changed relationships is therefore an important consideration in assessing a given family system.

The family system consists of a network of relationships, continually changing in response to stimulus from inside or outside the family. The family maintains its unity and viability throughout this process of change by achieving a balance in relationships. Maintaining a state of equilibrium or homeostasis is an essential process since the survival of the family depends upon this basic process.

Developing communication pathways. The family system relies heavily upon communication among family members to maintain relationships, define social roles, and cope with conflicts that threaten to disrupt the orderly functioning of the family unit. Communication is the process whereby one person sends a message to another person. The nature of communication appears simple enough at first sight. The process involves two persons: the sender and the receiver of the message. However, the sender is not always certain that the person who received the message correctly understood the intended meaning. At best words lack clarity and precision. Different meanings attach to the same word. Language can be subject to a number of different interpretations and two persons do not always attach the same meaning to a specific sentence. When messages are conveyed between family members, the possibility of misunderstanding or misinterpretation arises.

To make the communication process effective, family members need to be certain that they understand what is being expressed. Ambiguity clouds meanings, and family members are often confused by communications whose meanings have been obscured or hidden. Researchers who have studied patterns of communication in families that produce schizophrenic offspring have pointed out that communication pathways in these families are extremely confusing. The confusion results from the inability of family members to convey a single meaning in such a way that other family members can respond rationally. Moreover, verbal messages are accompanied by body language inconsistent with the verbal message, producing a "double bind" because the receiver must choose to respond to the verbal or the nonverbal part of the communication and cannot respond to both messages without ignoring one of them, hence a "double bind."

As Virginia Satir points out, "Absolutely clear communication is impossible to achieve because communication is, by its very nature incomplete. But there are degrees of incompleteness. The dysfunctional communicator leaves the receiver groping or guessing about what he has inside his head or heart" (Satir, 1968, p. 73). In families functional in communication, family members feel free to ask for clarification of unclear or confusing messages. This process of checking out the meaning of messages leads to a higher degree of mutual understanding and lays the groundwork for open and honest expression of thoughts and feelings. If family members do not feel free to ask for clarification, the groundwork is laid for future misunderstanding, confusion, and conflict.

In functional families, communication is used as an important vehicle for giving and receiving information, revealing and expressing feelings, and resolving differences among family members. Without an open communication system, the family has limited information upon which to make decisions, elicit feelings, or cope with conflict. An open communication system is one in which communications are reciprocal, with family members open to requests for clarification, and responses and exchanges between all members encouraged. As Francis Scherz points out, "Every interaction and transaction expressed in communication is reciprocal in nature, and in every communication the person is affected by the actions of others and they, in turn, are affected" (Scherz, 1970, p. 234).

One's ability to communicate clearly and effectively is a skill acquired from the family in which one lived as a child. Adults are the models for communication. They provide the blueprint as to how communication takes place and how it can be used or misused. "If the male and female who were his survival figures did not manage jointly, if their messages to each other and the child were unclear and contradictory, he himself will learn to communicate in an unclear and contradictory way," writes Satir (1968, p. 73).

Communication consists of more than written or spoken words. All behavior is a form of communication. Everything that a family member does in relation to another family member has meaning and conveys a message. Nonverbal expressions of feeling are, indeed, more often accurate and effective ways of communicating. Family members are alert to tone of voice, bodily posture, and facial expression because these nonverbal aspects of messages are often a more reliable basis for understanding their meaning. As Lederer and Jackson point out, communication takes on many forms.

> The raising of eyebrows, the bringing of flowers, the cooking of a favorite dessert, a handshake, a surly grumble, an unexpected holding of the hand, a kiss, all these are examples of nonverbal behavior that sends a message to another person. In relating to another person, it is impossible not to communicate. If one turns away or is silent, one conveys a message. The way one behaves, moves, holds oneself, all these transmit messages (Lederer and Jackson, 1968, p. 99).

Breakdown in communication is one of the most frequent causes of disruption of family systems. Family members may speak to one another, but neither hears what the other is saying. A habit of "non-listening" becomes established as the normal way of communicating. Since communication involves a two-way process, a breakdown occurs if one of the parties is not attending to what the other is saying. A second breakdown in communication occurs when the message sent is not the message received. Since any given message has more than one possible meaning, the meaning depends on the interpretation of the listener. That interpretation may be quite different from the meaning the speaker intended. Lederer and Jackson have called attention to how these misinterpretations may lead to increasing difficulties among family members.

> As soon as families begin to squabble, the number of messages incorrectly received increases. People who are quarreling fall into the trap of saying one thing when they mean another, or of hearing one thing when something else has been said, because they are angry, hurt, or frightened. It has often been remarked that none are so blind as those who will not see. Unfortunately, we may say that none are so deaf as those who will not hear (p. 281).

Coping with conflict. Conflict is an inevitable part of family living and can occur on several levels. There may be conflict between the family and the community. For example, school rules may conflict with parents over a child's conduct, and a conflict over the value of education may become a family issue. Or the extended family may be at odds with the nuclear family. Grandparents may actively interfere in the raising of the children and cause conflict to break out between husband and wife. Conflict may also grow out of one family member's attempt to develop an identity not accepted by other family members. Differences in life styles, values, and personal strivings constitute the most common sources of conflict within the family.

Efforts to resolve or control conflict can take several forms. In some cases, the family attempts to deny the existence of conflict. The very thought that there could be significant difference between husband and wife or between parents and children is so frightening that the system attempts to cover up any indication of conflict. Lyman Wynne refers to the phenomena of "pseudo-mutuality." In such families, differences are denied through "a type of surface alignment that blurs and obscures from recognition and conscious experience both underlying splits and divergences, on the one hand, and deeper affection and alignment on the other hand. Pseudo-mutuality involves a level of experience in which underlying unsettled business is 'settled' or fixed by a kind of alignment that forestalls further exploration of the relationship" (Wynne, 1961, p. 109).

If the family develops patterns that deny the existence of conflict, there is a strong possibility that the conflict will be driven underground and at some point take the form of a dysfunction in one or more family member. Ackerman points out that scapegoating may result from such forms of unresolved conflict. Since the family cannot cope with conflict in a rational manner, the emotional life of one family member suffers. This family member becomes the scapegoat or the victim of the family's inability to resolve conflict. This process of "scapegoating" may victimize a family pair or particular individual, according to Ackerman. "The victim may be a child, an adolescent, or an adult. The effects of such prejudice and scapegoating are of fundamental significance with regard to the unconscious selection of one or another member as the victim of emotional breakdown and mental illness" (Ackerman, 1961, p. 57).

Family therapists generally find that families are not aware of the underlying source of conflict in their relationships. Families do present areas in which differences arise such as money management, child-rearing practices or interference from in-laws. The question for the family therapist is: Why are these the areas of conflict and why is the family unable or unwilling to resolve the conflicts? The purpose of the family therapist is to help the family achieve a better understanding and clearer perception of the real source and nature of the conflict.

Underlying family conflict is the need for individuals within the family to be in a position of controlling other family members. Competition for positions of power generates and maintains the conflict, regardless of the specific issue involved. Each family member feels insecure unless he is in a position of superiority over other members. This struggle for superiority or for equality in status indicates a fear of inferiority, or at least a fear that others in the family do not consider each other as equals. Lederer and Jackson have referred to this struggle as "symmetrical behavior" and explain how it operates within a family system.

> The process of status struggle, or symmetrical behavior, usually starts when one person states or indicates an opinion, or specifies the way something should be done, or unilaterally initiates an action which involves both parties. The other person receives the message and concludes, "My spouse doesn't believe I am as good or skilled as he is. I don't like that — I am equal and probably superior (p. 164).

The source of conflict can often be traced to this struggle for power and position within the family system. Once the struggle begins, it tends to spread over more and more areas. The struggle for power then escalates into open and sometimes vicious conflict. Usually such battles continue indefinitely.

Conflict between husband and wife sometimes grows out of a childhood experience which has failed to provide models for resolving conflict. One parent was overly dominant and the other parent found ways of covertly and subtly undermining the dominant parent's position in the family. The child of such a union has no way of learning how to avoid the pattern to which s/he was exposed, and the struggle for a position of dominance over his or her mate continues. Or if any of the partners withdraws from the struggle, the conflict is driven underground where it becomes more difficult to resolve.

The process of growth and change that occurs during the family life cycle also produces conflict. The family attempts to deal with change by maintaining the status quo. But the family cannot stay the same. When the family system attempts to foreclose the possibility of change and refuses to accommodate to new situations, the conflict tends to escalate unless the system finds a method of adjusting to changed circumstances. "In the last analysis," writes Ackerman, "it is the pattern of coping with conflict that influences the relative balance to cling to the old and the urge to receive new experience. The control of conflict affects the family's capacity for growth. When the control of conflict fails or is decompensated, the excess of anxiety induces a more intense clinging to what is old, and reduces the ability to learn from new experience" (p. 59).

Healthy Families

The basic processes of family interaction take on characteristics that make it possible to distinguish between healthy families and troubled families. A recent study by Beavers and Lewis compared the families of disturbed adolescents with families in which there were no psychiatric symptoms. The comparison offered valuable findings about differences in family structure, communication, relationships and negotiation (Beavers, 1978).

Family structure. The coalition between parents is secure and unquestioned in healthy families. Power is in the parents' hands. But power is also shared between the father and the mother. Their decisions are reached through careful deliberation with the opinions of the children taken into account. Parents do not exercise their power in an authoritarian or arbitrary fashion, but once a decision has been reached, parents stick together in supporting what they have decided to be the course of action to follow. A strong parental coalition provides the family with the sense of leadership and confidence important to its survival. Moreover, the children in healthy families do not seem to resent parents' exercise of power because they feel that parents do respect and value them as individuals and their opinions are respectfully considered in coming to a decision. Therefore, the children accept the parents' authority with a minimum of rebellion; differences between father and mother do not result in serious splits within the family or weaken the effectiveness of its leadership.

This strong bond between parents provides the basis for unity and security in the family system. The family is not torn by alignments and splits between parents and children. There is also a feeling of closeness among family members in healthy families. They share a great deal of their feeling and ideas with one another. They have a sense of belonging, of being connected, of being part of a highly supportive network of relationships. Yet each family member has his own individual and unique space within the family system.

Autonomy. In healthy families, unity does not mean that individual family members completely submerge their own individuality in the interest of family solidarity. Autonomy is encouraged in healthy families. Along with a feeling of closeness, there is also a sense of separateness and individuality that permits self-expression. Differences in personality, in ideas, in life styles are not only accepted in healthy families, but strongly encouraged. Individual differences are recognized and accepted. Family members are able to make judgments on their own, and to separate their opinions from those of other family members. In these families, initiative is strongly valued and supported so that each family member has an opportunity to grow and develop his/her own potential and make maximum use of his/her special talents, capacities, and interests.

Communication. Personal autonomy is encouraged through communication. In healthy families, everyone is permitted to express his/her feelings clearly and openly. Through the clear expression of ideas, feelings, and problems family members are able to establish their own personal identities. As Lewis points out, family members are able to establish boundaries between themselves and other family members. "Children raised in families in which there is a strong pull for the clear definition of what each individual feels and thinks are exposed to a powerful, day-to-day training program in defining where one's own skin ends and other's begins" (Lewis, 1976, p. 212).

Healthy families show a high degree of permeability. Each family member is willing to acknowledge what other members feel or think, and all are open to and receptive to what others are saying. Each person is treated as important. Permeability must be distinguished from invasiveness. Invasiveness is found in families that intrude on the autonomy of the individual member by speaking for him or her, rather than permitting the individual speak for him- or herself. Invasiveness is therefore the enemy of autonomy and defeats efforts at defining one's own identity. Lewis describes the important difference between families that encourage autonomy and those that are unable to achieve autonomy:

> Children brought up in families who communicate unclearly, have low levels of responsibility, are impermeable, and invade frequently will have much more difficulty achieving autonomy. Children raised in families who speak clearly, encourage responsibility, and rarely

invade will, on the average, achieve automony with fewer
difficulties (p. 72).

Negotiation. The viability and health of a family depends on an
ability to resolve differences quickly and to perform tasks efficiently.
Families that are healthy show a capacity to do both. If differences
arise, family members develop a method for dealing with the issues
in the early stages and avoiding long delays during which decisions
are left hanging and conflicts remain unresolved. Input from all
family members is invited in resolving differences, and the family
attempts to come up with a solution satisfactory to everyone whenever possible. The ability to negotiate is also an indication that the
family can solve problems with a minimum of difficulty. When
confronted with a problem, the family searches for consensus, engages
in give and take and is willing to make compromises to achieve a
workable agreement. Healthy families are able to accept direction
and organize themselves to respond to a task. They identify problems early and confront them directly before they worsen. Rather
than trying to determine who's to blame for a mistake, healthy
families consider what needs to be done about a problem.

The ability to negotiate and to perform tasks is a special asset
in times of crisis. Even crises such as serious illness or death, difficult as they may be, can be surmounted. Problems in interpersonal
relations that threaten to split the family apart can be resolved and
the unity of the family can be preserved. Once a plan of action has
been agreed upon the family is ready to go into action and bring
about a resolution of the problem. In seeking a solution to a recognized difficulty, the family explores various possibilities. The ability
of the healthy family to remain flexible in response to a crisis is
a major factor in problem-solving. Closed systems shut out new
input and information and meet every problem in the same way. The
responses to stress are extremely limited. Healthy family systems
are open systems. They are capable of changing responses and meeting new problems in new ways. As Lewis points out, these families
do not depend on any one family member to solve a problem or
cope with a crisis. Power is shared in healthy families; all family
members are capable of bringing their individual resources to bear
on the solution of a family difficulty. "Their openness to each
family member's perceptions and opinions leads to clarification of
a shared reality. They can seek general agreement about the nature of
the stress and everyone can play a part in the effort to deal with
it" (p. 136).

In summary, the healthy family is capable of functioning in the following ways:

● The family structure provides for a sharing of power between parents who give strong leadership to the family. There is a strong tie that binds the parents in a coalition. The family is not split by a continuing struggle for power. The structure of the family provides a high degree of solidarity that makes for stability.

● Healthy family systems encourage a high degree of autonomy and independence among family members. Healthy families can appreciate and accept differences and do not view individual expressions of feelings and ideas as threats to the family's well-being.

● Healthy families have developed effective methods of communication. Family members are capable of expressing their ideas and perceptions of one another cleary and freely. Communication is open and honest. Family members are receptive to others and value the input that each member contributes to the life of the family.

● Healthy families are effective in coping with problems and dealing with crisis situations quickly and efficiently. These families recognize problems early, are able to develop alternative solutions and decide on a course of action.

● Healthy families are skilled in the process of negotiation. They have developed an ability to resolve differences in the interest of the family's well-being and are willing to work out compromises that are satisfactory through a rational process of give and take.

Troubled Families
Healthy families, like all families, encounter trouble at various points, but they are not constantly under stress. At the opposite end of the spectrum are those families that have serious difficulty in almost every area of functioning. They are the troubled families that produce mental illness and serious behavior disorders. They include families often in a state of conflict that produces constant warfare within the family. They also include chaotic families that are highly disorganized and produce symptoms found in schizophrenic patients whose thinking processes are severely disordered and out of touch with reality. The contrast between these troubled families and healthy families becomes apparent when the two systems are compared in regard to power structure, autonomy, communication and negotiation *(see Table 2.1)*.

Table 2.1. *Family Functioning Spectrum.*

	Healthy Families	Mid-range Families	Troubled Families
Power structure	Strong parental coalition Power shared by parents	One parent dominates other parent Parents compete for power	Neither parent provides leadership Chaos results
Autonomy	Members have clear boundaries Autonomy valued and encouraged	Autonomy is limited Submission to others encouraged	Vague and poorly defined boundaries Members lack self-identity
Communication Patterns	Clear expression of feelings Open communication pattern	Clear communication System closed, with one-way pattern	Messages confused Attempts to clarify meanings fail
Negotiation patterns	Decisions arrived at quickly Input from others is welcomed Tasks performance is is efficient	Decisions made by dominant parent Little opportunity for negotiation	Severe difficulties in negotiation Unable to perform and carry out tasks

Power structure. The power structure of troubled families takes one of the following basic forms. In some troubled families, one person, most often the husband, exerts all the power in the family and controls all other family members, relegating the other parent to a childlike position. In some situations, the person who holds and exercises power is not challenged directly. Attempts to undermine his or her control are indirect and underground. In other families, there is open rebellion against the controling family member. Chaotic families are out of control. Parents in chaotic families abrogate their roles as family leaders. Older children sometimes attempt to take over the reins, and dominate both parents and siblings. In some troubled families, there is a constant parental struggle for power. Neither parent is willing to share power. They cannot develop any way of reaching decisions or of making compromises in the interest of family well-being. In all cases, the family suffers from the lack of the strong coalition between the parents found in healthy families. The leadership to which the family looks for guidance and control is based upon a need to gain power rather than to solve problems. In chaotic families, no one has sufficient power to provide leadership and the system begins to fall apart.

Autonomy. Troubled families have very serious problems in developing a sense of autonomy in family members. A family dominated by one of the parents creates a system of relations that does not permit the free expression of opinions not in harmony with those of the dominant parent. The power structure of the family dictates a hierarchy, rather than an open system in which the views, thoughts, and feelings of others are regarded as valuable and the dignity of each family member is respected.

In conflicted family systems the problem of autonomy is never resolved, since both parents are struggling for dominance. In this struggle for control, the children are drawn into the continuous pattern of marital conflict. Under these conditions, the possibility of developing strong feelings of intimacy and affection in the offspring are absent. There are temporary alignments of children with one of the parents, but these attachments do not endure since they are based upon a desire to be on the "winning side" in the war between the parents. As Lewis points out, "The parents lead lives that, in many ways, have a bitter and desperate quality. The children are either dragged into the conflict or early in life give up hope of finding happiness within the family and begin to distance themselves from the family scene" (p. 128).

Autonomy is also most difficult to achieve in chaotic families. There is an unspoken rule that everyone should and must have the same opinion, think alike and feel alike. Murray Bowen refers to this phenomena as the "undifferentiated family ego mass" that lies at the root of families that produce schizophrenic reaction in one of the family members. Lyman Wynn refers to this sense or need for "we-ness" in these families as "psuedo-mutuality" because the family seeks to block out any expression of individuality. Studies of these chaotic families indicate that boundaries between family members are not clearly defined. There is a highly symbiotic tie between family members that prevents the development of a mature, independent person, and children who grow up in these families have difficulty in coping with the problems of the adult world.

Communication. Problems in communication are more serious in chaotic families than in dominant or conflicted families. The communication processes of the schizophrenic family have been studied in some detail in an attempt to unravel the complexity of the schizophrenic's pattern of trying to make connection with others. Ineffective communication causes these families to be in a constant state of chaos and unreality. Confused and contradictory messages obscure family differences and problems rather than resolve them. The verbal meaning of a message is often denied by the nonverbal message so that the communication results in complete meaninglessness: Bateson's double bind. Family members are unable to risk clear communication because it might endanger or disturb the balance (or homeostasis) that the family system relies upon to keep it intact. Lewis describes how these families communicate.

> Communication is difficult to follow and the flow of ideas in a family conversation's meaning are thus obscured. Often members appear not to hear each other; at other times they seem to use a private language. Problems are often totally disregarded. A child's mental illness may be brushed aside with, "It's only nervousness — it will disappear," until outsiders point out hallucinations, delirious, or bizarre behavior. Feelings are frequently denied and some chaotic families have a flat, monotonous quality. The prevailing family mood may involve despair, hopelessness or cynicism (p. 129).

Negotiation and problem-solving. The family with a dominant parent provides little or no opportunity for negotiation. Since these families are very rigidly controled, they have difficulty adjusting to problems that accompany change. The dominant parent is all powerful and rules are held to be inflexible. The family system is closed, and is not subject to influence from the "outside world." Growing up in this type family can produce a variety of symptoms: excessively shy and withdrawn persons, rebels who come into conflict with authority, or depressed and fearful. This type of family probably produces a fairly large percentage of the families from which the mentally ill originate.

The conflicted family certainly does not offer its members any experience in negotiation, since issues are never settled on a basis of give and take but rather on who can gain power over the other. They tend to produce offspring "prone to behavior that will be labeled as 'sociopathic' and, as often happens, will be in jail rather than in psychiatric hospitals" (Beavers, 1977, p. 44). The conflicted family also makes it difficult for the offspring to develop a capacity for intimacy, and problems in interpersonal relationships are the result of this inability to relate to others, to be sensitive to the feelings of others, or to trust others. The lack of these abilities is what produces behavior destructive to the self and to others. Beavers describes this experience:

> Most often the sociopath develops in a family which offers little affirmation of tenderness, gentleness, and honest expression of vulnerability. . . . In a family structure with shifting power, incoherent communication, and overall rejection of the tender and vulnerable, a child finds no way to be loved by obeying rules, no behavior patterns that are consistently rewarded by closeness and caring. . . . Experience in the primary family teaches the sociopath-to-be that his feelings, impulses, and needs are so unacceptable that he must be forever outside the warmth of human relationship systems (Beavers, 1977, p. 74).

Chaotic families have serious problems in task performance and problem-solving. These families are incapable of completing a simple task such as planning an outing because the communication process is highly ineffective in dealing with reality. Digressions lead the family astray. Concentration on a minor detail becomes a matter of great concern and long deliberation. "Goal direction is lost and the family wallows like a rudderless ship," writes Beavers. "These families rarely

succeed in deciding among themselves what to plan, and they often stop
working on the task entirely and begin to discuss past events or dreams
of the distant future'' (p. 49). The chaotic family produces individuals
incapable of dealing with reality or of making sound judgments because the family system has been unable to deal with the important
functions of encouraging autonomy, establishing clear boundaries,
and developing clear and effective methods of communication.

In summary, a comparison of troubled families to healthy families
leads to these conclusions:

● Power is not shared in troubled families. In troubled families
there is a weak coalition between parents. One parent is dominant and
the other is submissive, or each parent is struggling to gain power over
the other. In chaotic families there is a marked absence of leadership.

● Autonomy is not adequately developed in dysfunctional, troubled
families. Boundaries between family members are defined too rigidly
in some troubled families. In the chaotic families, the boundaries are
so vague that there is a loss of self-identity.

● Communication is either constricted or distorted in troubled
families. Some have problems communicating feelings, and the development of intimacy among family members is severely limited.
Chaotic families, unable to communicate clearly, become confused
in their attempts to resolve problems.

● Troubled families that involve conflict between parents have difficulty in negotiating differences and resolving internal conflicts.
Chaotic families have serious problems in coping with reality and
lack the leadership necessary to help the family deal with crisis.

The above factors were cited in the Timberlawn study which compared functional family systems to dysfunctional family sytems (Beavers, 1977). The research suggests that family systems tend to arrange
themselves along a continuum from highly functional healthy families
to severely troubled family systems that are exceedingly dysfunctional.
The healthy families produce autonomous, symptom-free individuals.
Severely dysfunctional family systems produce fairly serious forms of
psychopathology. Chaotic families produce schizophrenic symptoms.
Serious behavior disorders or depressive states are also found in dysfunctional families. Between the extremes of optimal families and
severely dysfunctional families are the mid-range systems that do not
produce serious psychopathology or behavior disturbances. The mid-
range families are mildly dysfunctional, produce neurotic personality
patterns, but are able to function fairly adequately. Dissatisfaction in

Table 2.2. *Psychiatric Symptoms and Family Systems.*

Healthy Families	Mid-range Families	Troubled Families
Symptom-free	Neuroses	Schizophrenia
Optimal functioning	Depression	Serious behavior disorders
High degree of autonomy	Borderline adjustment	Sociopathic personality disorders
	Mild behavior disorders	

the relationship between husband and wife is found in mid-range families. There are feelings of disappointment and expressions of disillusionment about the marriage in these families. Problems in developing strong bonds of intimacy between the partners are characteristic *(see Table 2.2)*.

Assessing Family Systems

In making an assessment of family functioning, the following outline serves as a guide for gathering significant information.

I. Stages in the Family Life Cycle

An assessment of how the family is functioning at a given stage in the life cycle (early marriage, expansion, consolidation, or contraction of the family), and the problems closely related to a specific stage.

A. ● How compatible are the partners sexually at this stage?
   ● Are the emotional needs of each being met by the other partner?
   ● Is there some fairly well-agreed-upon definition of roles of each partner?

B. ● How are the partners working out agreements about birth control, child care, and handling rivalry between the siblings?
   ● Are there financial problems that go unresolved?
   ● Is there agreement about the wife going to work? About changes in the husband's employment?

C. ● How are the family members adjusting to the addition of children to the family circle? To children leaving the family to enter school or to marry?

II. Family's Social Environment

An assessment of the neighborhood and community in which the family lives and the impact of the social environment on the life of family members.

A. ● What are the dominant characteristics of the neighborhood?
   ● Is is relatively safe or dangerous?
   ● What is the relationship between the family and others in the immediate vicinity?

B. ● What facilities does the community provide for health care? Education? Police protection? Recreation?

C. ● What is the position of the family in the social structure?
   ● What are the possibilities for upward mobility?

D. ● What impact does the environment have on the physical well-being of the family?
   ● On the mental health of family members?

III. Family Structure and Processes

An assessment of the internal functioning of the family system with special attention to each of the following areas of the family system:

A. *Family structure*. An assessment of how power is structured and the position of individuals within the family system. The following questions are raised in this area of family functioning:

● Which family member(s) are dominant and hold the most power?
● Do parents form a strong coalition?
● Is there a "power struggle" between the parents?
● Are family members split into factions, some who have power and others who are "left out"?

B. *Autonomy and independence*. An assessment of how the system deals with problems of autonomy, independence, and maturation of its members. The following issues are raised:

● Are family members encouraged to express feelings and ideas?
● Are boundaries between family members defined too rigidly or too vaguely?
● Do individual family members have freedom to pursue their special interests and develop their potential?
● Do they have a strong sense of personal self-identity?

C. *Communication patterns*. An assessment of how family members communicate with one another to negotiate and to complete tasks. The following are matters that require exploration:

- How does the system provide opportunities for exchange of messages between family members?
- Are the messages clearly expressed? Is their meaning clearly perceived?
- Are some limits put on what may and may not be expressed?
- Is communication successful in resolving conflict? Accomplishing a task?

D. *Negotiation processes*. The assessment involves a study of how the family negotiates conflict and differences among its members, and raises the following questions:

- What is the family's typical approach to resolving conflict?
- In what areas does negotiation take place? Does not take place?
- Who initiates the negotiation process?
- How successful are the family's attempts at negotiation?

E. *Coping with problems*. This part of the assessment involves the ability of the family to cope with stress such as loss of a family member, changes in life situation, or loss of income.

- Does the family have a flexible and varied approach to dealing with crisis?
- How does the family attempt to restore equilibrium and adapt to change?
- What mechanisms does the family employ in coping with problems (denial, projection, etc.)
- What supportive resources are available in the family's social network (relatives, friends, neighbors, etc.)

The assessment of the family is based upon a social study that includes data on all of the above areas of family functioning. The application of this approach is illustrated in the following case study.

Baker Family. Sixteen year old Betty was referred to a social service agency in a mid-western city after she announced that she was planning to drop out of high school in her sophomore year. Her grades were quite satisfactory, and her announcement came as a surprise to her parents who had assumed that Betty would certainly finish high school and perhaps go on to college to prepare for a teaching career.

In the first family session, the mother disclaimed any further responsibility for Betty's future. "All my life I've been the one who has had to worry about Betty. Well, I'm not going to keep on worrying about you," she said turning to Betty. "It's time someone else in this family takes over some of the responsibility. I've done it long enough." She turned to her husband. Betty's father remained silent.

"Well, Dad never finished high school and he did okay. So why can't I do the same thing. What's so important about getting an education anyway?" Betty turned to her mother. "Just because you are going back to college, doesn't mean everyone else has to do the same thing. I don't have to be just like you. So if I want to quit school, there is no law that says I can't."

The family remained silent. Mother was obviously irritated. She stared straight ahead. Betty's brother Billy squirmed and glanced in his father's direction. Mr. Baker broke the silence. He turned to the therapist, "I don't know much about this. Education is not something I guess I can talk about. My wife is always the one who looks after these matters. She is the expert, you know. I've kept out of this whole argument between Betty and her mother. Now my wife wants me to take over and tell Betty she has to stay in school. For sixteen years she has had charge of Betty and I never interfered. I thought she wanted it that way. Now she tells me to take over — after sixteen years."

The initial family session provided some significant information about the power structure in the Baker family. Mother and father had not shared responsibility equally. Somewhat by default, the father had given over his share of responsibility for Betty to his wife. The split between the parents had occurred early in Betty's life. Mr. Baker had withdrawn early on from his wife and his daughter. He explained that his wife made him feel that he did not know much about being a father, was highly critical of him, and caused him to feel inferior because of his lack of formal education.

A year ago, Mrs. Baker had enrolled in college. She had plans for getting a degree in business administration. This decision to return to school seemed to contribute to the family's problems as Mrs. Baker's interest in school took more of her time and energy. The mother had been the parent who provided leadership and direction for the family. Now she was interested in developing her own career. The family system was undergoing change and imbalanced, and Betty's assertion of her own autonomy at the same time that her mother was moving away from her earlier role complicated the problem.

When Mrs. Baker announced that someone else in the family should start being a parent, she was attempting to resolve the imbalance in the family system by putting the father in charge of Betty. Mr. Baker was resisting this shift in the power structure. The mother's control had been close to absolute. Mr. Baker played a very minor role as parent. Now that Mrs. Baker was moving out of her role as the dominant parent, the family was leaderless, and had moved from a structure in which there was a high degree of dominance to a state bordering on chaos.

There was a very weak coalition between the parents. But there were some underlying coalitions between parents and children. The son, Billy, had never been in a close relation with his father. Mr. Baker recounted that he had tried to interest Billy in the scouts and had even taken on responsibility as a scoutmaster, hoping that "this would bring me and Billy closer, but it didn't seem to work." Instead, Billy preferred to read and took considerable pride in being an outstanding student in his eighth grade class. Billy received much praise and approval from his mother for his academic achievements.

Betty felt as though she had never come up to her mother's expectations in her school performance. Her grades were B + to average — not high enough to bring favorable comment from her mother. Betty felt sorry for Dad. He works hard, she said, but he never got much appreciation for his efforts to provide a modest but steady income for the family. Betty saw her mother's return to college as just another example of how Mrs. Baker wanted to "lord it over Dad." Betty also sensed that her brother, Billy, was the mother's favorite child.

Family members do find it possible to communicate their feelings about themselves and others in a fairly clear way. The mother states her view about her own need for autonomy and self-realization. She also expresses her feelings about her husband's lack of concern in regard to Betty and how she feels about having had to bear major responsibility for parenting and leadership in the past. The father also expresses feelings about his relationship to his wife, but his messages are less clear in regard to his daughter. Mr. Baker tends to respond to messages from his wife by making references to the past, blaming the family's present state on the mother who undermined his role and influence on the daughter. Mr. Baker also expresses a sense of inadequacy and inferiority, a rather shaky image of himself, but again presents himself as a martyr who has suffered humiliation from his wife.

The daughter, Betty, speaks out rather clearly about her desire for autonomy and her need to make decisions in regard to her own life without interference from her mother. Betty also reveals her feelings about the mother's domination of the father. Her defense of the father indicates that Betty may identify her problem as being the same one the father has been trying to cope with, namely, his submissive relationship to his wife. Betty symbolizes the need for autonomy in her adolescent rebellion against the mother who embodies the repressive and critical parent figure. Her announcement that she will quit school and that no one can force her to continue her education represents a fairly typical adolescent striving for independence from parental authority and her efforts to establish her own identity independent of her mother.

The father tends to blame the mother for the family's problem in that Mrs. Baker has always assumed the management of the children. He does not refer to his part in bringing about this situation, explaining his withdrawal from leadership as due to efforts to please his wife. In this connection, he speaks for his wife, or more accurately, he says what he believes to have been in his wife's mind, namely, that she did not want him to interfere in the relationship and difficulties between her and Betty.

The daughter's expression of hostility toward her mother is fairly direct. The father's and mother's expression of hostility toward each other is more guarded and expressed indirectly. The overall affect in the family sometimes borders on a state of depression and hopelessness. At other times, there are expressions of a desire for more warmth and affection as found in the father's attempt to draw close to Billy in the past, in Betty's sympathy for her father, and her appreciation of his steadfastness in providing for the family's physical well-being.

In assessing the Baker family, one finds areas in which there are indications of some dysfunctioning. The lack of a strong coalition between the parents is a major problem and weakens the family system. Expressions of feeling and open communication is an asset and is an indication that the family members can move in the direction of resolving the crisis that arose when the daughter threatened to quit school in spite of her parent's disapproval. The ability of the family to move in this direction will be tested as they progress through the treatment process.

References

Ackerman, N. (Ed.) *Exploring the base for family therapy*. New York: Family Service Association of America, 1961.

Bateson, G., Jackson, D., Haley, J. & Weakland, J. Toward a theory of schizophrenia. *Behavior Science*, 1956, *1*, 251-264.

Beavers, W. R. *Psychotherapy and growth*. New York: Brunner/Mazel, 1977.

Beck, D. *Progress on family problems*. New York: Family Service Association of America, 1973.

Hollingshead, A. *Social class and mental illness*. New York: John Wiley, 1958.

Lederer, W., & Jackson, D. *The mirages of marriage*. New York: W. W. Norton, 1968.

Lewis, J. M., et al. *No single thread: Psychological health in family systems*. New York: Brunner/Mazel, 1976.

Satir, V. *Conjoint family therapy*. Palo Alto: Science and Behavior, 1968.

Scherz, F. "Theory and practice of family therapy" in Roberts, R. *Theories of social casework*. Chicago: Chicago University Press, 1970.

Wynne, L. "The study of intrafamilial alignments and splits in exploratory family therapy," in N. Ackerman, (Ed.) *Exploring the base for family therapy*. New York: Family Service Association of America, 1961.

THREE

Approaches to Helping

Helping troubled families cope with problems in relationships requires a high level of professional competence in social work practice. During the past two decades, social workers and related helping professionals have developed new approaches to working with troubled families. These approaches include the use of behavior modification, crisis intervention, family therapy and social networking. An understanding of the basic principles that underlie these approaches and a knowledge of how each approach can be used in working with families will make it possible for social workers to carry out their role more effectively and efficiently.

Behavioral Social Work

The use of behavior modification by social workers is a recent innovation designed to help clients with a variety of problems. Although the techniques used in behavior modification appear complicated, the goal of this method of helping can be stated in simple terms: to bring about an increase in desired behavior and to decrease undesired behavior. The application of the behavioral approach to working with families involves these basic procedures: evaluating the presented problem; observing and surveying behavior; specifying target behavior and establishing priorities as to behaviors to be changed.

Evaluating and assessing the problem that the family presents involves an inquiry into what behavioral changes the family wants to make and determining if such changes would result in helping the family function more adequately. The assessment of the family also requires careful observation of the processes of interaction among family members to determine how the various persons in the environment contribute to or maintain certain forms of behavior. After these observations, the specific behavior to be changed is spelled out in detail, and this specific behavior becomes the target behavior that will be the focus of the social worker and the family during treatment. The choice of target behavior depends on several factors, and is usually determined by mutual agreement between the social worker and the family. After assessment, when the target behavior has been identified, the social worker determines the techniques to be used in bringing about behavior change. In most cases, the objective will be to increase desirable behavior, rather than to decrease objectionable behavior. That is, the techniques of positive reinforcement are used whenever possible.

Family members' cooperation is absolutely essential if behavior modification is to achieve the goals set out at the beginning of working with a family problem. This is especially important in bringing about changes in the area of parent/child relationships because one or both parents are the persons in the child's environment who will be called upon to apply the specific techniques designed to change the objectionable behavior of the child. The parent is carefully instructed as to how to apply the techniques of behavior modification in a very specific, planned process over a given period of time. In taking the role of mediator, the parent must carry out the plan consistently and with great precision. The mediator must be someone strongly motivated to bring about behavior change, instructed in how to modify behavior, and who is present most of the time during which the objectionable behavior occurs. Usually one or both parents work with the social worker and under the social worker's guidance and instruction as mediator.

Changing parent/child interaction. Behavior modification in the home, with the parents acting as the change agent, has been used as an effective way of helping the family bring about changes and modify habitual processes of interaction between the child and his parents. The overall objective is to train the parents in the use of behavior modification and to give specific instructions that they will be required to carry out. In applying the behavioral approach, the social worker makes a contract with the parents that states the specific behavior to be changed and specifies who will be responsible for carrying out the behavior modification program. The contract also sets forth the time necessary to bring about the desired changes and what is to be the result in terms of behavior change.

The success of the intervention in the family generally depends heavily on the commitment of the mediator (usually the parent) to bring about changes. Even more important the mediator must be effective and knowledgeable about the modification process. Therefore, the social worker should spend a good deal of time explaining the techniques to be employed and how they are to be used. How the parent can play an important therapeutic role in changing interaction patterns is illustrated in the following case example described by Hawkins (1966).

Peter, age four, was brought to the clinic because his mother found it very difficult to control temper outbursts during which he would kick, scream, and tear his clothing. She reported that Peter demanded her constant attention and that he became extremely angry at the slightest frustration. Observation of Peter's behavior at home made it clear that the mother was maintaining the objectionable behavior. When Peter threw a tantrum, she would sometimes tell him he was behaving badly, and try to distract him by offering food or giving him a toy. At other times she would place him in his high chair for a short period of time; none of these measures brought about any significant change in the boy's behavior.

The techniques put into practice to change Peter's behavior included the following: the mother was simply to tell Peter to stop his objectionable behavior. If he continued his temper tantrum, the mother was to put him in his room and force him to remain there for a minimum of five minutes before he could come out. All playthings were removed from his room so that he would have no way of amusing himself. This method of controling Peter's behavior was continued for six sessions under the social worker's supervision. Then the mother continued to apply the ''time-out'' procedure on her own. A follow-up study showed that Peter's objectionable behavior had been reduced substantially, and the mother reported that he was less demanding and now well-behaved. The study also indicated that the relationship between Peter and his mother changed considerably. The mother's behavior became more kindly and accepting due to the changes brought about when the mother used a different approach to dealing with his temper tantrums.

Changing marital interaction. Families that present problems in marital relationships can also benefit from a behavioral approach to resolving problems in areas of difficulty or conflict. In most cases, each spouse feels that s/he is investing more in the relationship than the other. Each believes that s/he is receiving less in return for the investment in the marriage. The behavioral approach seeks to bring about a balance between what each partner gives and what each receives through a process of negotiation and contracting. The social worker helps the couple to form exchange contracts that require some changes in the behavior of both partners. Each is required to alter his or her behavior in such a way that positive, rewarding results will follow. The changes in behavior become positive reinforcers that maintain a mutually satisfying exchange and become the basis for a change in their relationship.

The first stage consists of making an assessment of various aspects of the marriage to determine in what respects the relationship fails to meet each partner's expectations. This survey leads to identification of those specific behaviors that each finds objectionable and a statement as to which behaviors are desired. The assessment phase also includes an assessment of what resources each partner has to offer to the other; love, status, money, service, praise, approval and expressions of caring. This inventory helps the couple recognize the resources that each regards as important and serves as a basis for exchange in the bargaining process to follow. This bargaining process is designed to teach the couple to use cooperative negotiating skills so they will be able to deal with marital conflict more effectively. The processes involved include the following:

- identifying problems areas;
- locating specific issues;
- generating and evaluating a variety of solutions;
- implementing the solutions to which they agree;
- evaluating the results.

Initially, the couple is taught how to communicate clearly and openly before contracting is attempted, and each partner is required to summarize what the other has said before stating his or her views and opinions. After this pattern of communication has been well established, the couple is asked to locate an aspect of their relationship they wish to improve. The emphasis is placed on a mutual problem that can become the focus of a joint effort toward resolution. At this point each partner is asked to explore the ways in which s/he is contributing to the problem by specific forms of behavior. This examination by the partners helps the couple identify those behaviors that need to be changed if a solution is to be reached and the relationship between them is to improve.

After the problematic behavior has been defined, each spouse is encouraged to think of ways in which it can be improved. A variety of possible alternative solutions is usually encouraged to increase the probability that the couple will discover one acceptable to both. This process also helps the couple become more flexible and creative in their problem-solving efforts. After the alternative solutions have been put forth, the partners are required to evaluate each solution, debating the pros and cons, and eventually coming to an agreement on which alternative they want to try.

Once the couple come to an agreement as to the exchanges to be made, a contract is arranged between them. The contract includes a statement as to what behaviors are expected, where they are to be performed, at what times and with what frequency. The contract may also specify penalties to be imposed if one or the other fails to carry out the contract's terms. After the contract has been spelled out, the couple embarks on a trial period in which they put the agreement into practice. They are asked to note when the contract is successful and when they find that they fail to carry out their agreement. The record of their experience in contracting is reviewed at each treatment session to determine whether any changes should be made in light of their experiences. The couple may then consider developing new alternatives and negotiating a new contract if they feel that renegotiation would be beneficial.

In order for the couple to profit from a behavioral approach to resolving marital conflict, certain prerequisites must be present, including the following:

- Both spouses should express a willingness to bargain, compromise and change their behavior to improve the marriage.
- Each partner must have something that the other partner values and that can be used as a basis for exchange in the bargaining process.
- Both partners must be willing to keep a record of their behavior (using graphs, charts and diaries) to evaluate progress.

If these conditions are not present, it is not likely that the behavioral approach will succeed in helping the couple arrive at a solution to their problem. Even if the conditions are met, some special training in communication and negotiation is often required before contracting can take place because successful exchanges of behavior can take place only if both partners are able to communicate their thoughts, feelings, needs, and expectations freely and honestly.

The behavioral approach is one that social workers can use effectively to improve family functioning, change parent/child interaction patterns and help couples resolve marital conflict. Because the effectiveness of behavior modification places great responsibility on the practitioner in influencing behavior, it is essential that the family perceives the goal of treatment to be in their best interest and are fully willing to participate in the change efforts.

Crisis Intervention

Families go through various types of crisis during their life cycles that tend to produce stress for the family members and that require accommodation to changes in the family system. Some crisis situations can be anticipated. For example, the birth of the first child, the adjustment to the empty nest after the last child leaves home, and the problems related to aging and death. Other crises, such as accidental death or the house burning down, come like bolts from the blue. There are also retroactive stresses, as in cases involving the revelation of old secrets or past events. Most families are able to resolve a crisis by taking some form of action to bring about a change in family roles or relationships. Other families do not resolve crises easily. At times of crisis they avoid making the necessary changes. Instead, some member of the family becomes a scapegoat and is placed under an unusual amount of personal strain and stress. Or the family unit itself may become so severely disorganized that a major step such as the placement of children in foster care or institutionalization of an adult family member is required.

Crisis intervention is an approach usually effective in helping families cope with crisis. The purpose of this form of intervention is to restore the family to normal functioning as quickly as possible by resolving the crisis immediately, so that the family system will remain intact and individual family members will experience a minimum amount of pain and emotional disequilibrium. Certain basic principles apply to this approach in helping troubled families.

- Crisis intervention is focused on the present problem the family is facing and the specific event that precipitated the crisis.
- Crisis intervention is reality oriented; the attention of the family is centered on a clear and realistic perception of what has happened and what measures are to be undertaken to resolve the conflict.

- Crisis intervention is short-term and time-limited and the family is required to take steps to resolve the crisis within a relatively short period of time.
- Crisis intervention requires the use of non-traditional means to help the family and an ability to employ an immediately effective pragmatic approach.
- Crisis intervention is designed to help the family develop adaptive coping mechanisms to enable its members deal with future crisis situations more effectively.

The techniques of crisis intervention have been employed in helping families cope with a variety of problems in several different settings. For example, a family may be faced with a teenage daughter who has run away from home and become involved in the drug scene. Or an adolescent son is arrested and held in detention for stealing a car and wrecking it while the police were in hot pursuit. Or an adult family member is being treated in the local hospital after attempting to commit suicide. Or sudden illness may strike the father in the form of a heart attack; while he hovers between life and death in the intensive care unit, the family's future hangs in the balance. At such critical junctures in family life immediate and effective help is needed to help the members cope with the stress and the sense of helplessness involved.

How the crisis intervention approach can help the troubled family is demonstrated in the work of the Family Treatment Unit at Colorado Psychiatric Hospital between 1964 and 1969. The unit, composed of a psychiatrist, social worker and nurse, was engaged in an effort to keep patients out of the psychiatric hospital while providing crisis therapy for the patient's family. Most of the patients included in the crisis intervention program were adolescents or young to middle-aged adults, from working- or lower-class families, diagnosed as schizophrenic or depressed.

The treatment unit proceeded on the theory that a psychiatric symptom in a family member was related to a crisis that had occurred within the patient's family. Therefore the team met with the entire family from the outset of their contact with the patient. The team's purpose in meeting with the patient's family was to help its members define the patient's symptoms as a family problem, rather than a problem for the psychotic or depressed individual family member. From the beginning, the team explains that there is some connection between events that have occurred within the family and the patient's symptoms. "In all cases, symptoms must be made coherent to the family," the unit points out. "In other words, symptoms are seen as arising from the crisis with the family, not as arising from incomprehensible conflicts within the patient'' (Pittman, 1971, p. 265).

In the early phase of working with the family, the therapist helps the family understand the patient's behavior, and points out that the chaos they are experiencing is temporary, that treatment will not be prolonged, and that the team is standing ready to deal with the crisis in a competent, effective way. These measures relieve the anxiety and uncertainty that the family is experiencing and are the prelude to the next step in helping the family cope with the crisis. Then the entire family is instructed to return home, taking the patient with them.

At this point, specific tasks are assigned to various family members. They are asked to do something that involves returning to functioning in a normal way, making a commitment to solving the crisis, or even making some specific change directly related to what produced the crisis in the first place. Tasks can include the performance of a somewhat fearsome task, such as making a telephone call to an employer or a more complicated task such as taking a school-phobic child back to school. Or the task can be a sort of truce about some unresolved conflict. In one family, the mother had refused to cook for the family because the husband refused to fix the washing machine. The family was assigned two tasks. The mother was told to clean the kitchen and the son was told to call the washing machine repairman. The team found that when the taks were completed the situation improved. Each family member had something tangible to do and was concerned with carrying out a specific task rather than continually blaming the patient for unusual behavior.

An important phase in family crisis intervention involves helping family members work together in negotiating solutions in areas of conflict. During these negotiations, one family member may deny involvement in the problem, or deny any necessity to interact with other family members in a different way. However, usually one member is able to help the therapist bring about changes in family relationships and this member can often be an effective ally in breaking through the family's resistance to change. In some cases the resistance cannot be easily overcome. In such situations it may be wise to simply make certain recommendations to the family, terminate the intervention, and let the family approach the matter of putting the recommendations into effect when they are ready. When termination approaches, the team assures the family of its availability for help in handling future crisis situations.

Brief intensive treatment of family crises that involve problems of adolescent psychopathology and behavior has also proven to be an effective approach to helping troubled families. This model, referred to as Multiple Impact Therapy, was developed by MacGregor and his associates as an alternative to long-term therapy for adolescents and their families, many of whom lived in communities where no such treatment was available. The multiple impact process of helping is based on two major assumptions: First, those families who face a crisis situation that may require institutional care of a disturbed adolescent are stimulated to mobilize their energies to cope with the problem. Second, intensive therapy offered at the outset is more useful to the family than traditional long-term of therapy models. Therefore, the intervention into the family system focuses on the immediate problem with a view to helping the family effect changes very rapidly and to sustaining the gains made during the treatment process.

The multiple impact model is based on the notion that an adolescent's "troubled" behavior is an expression of an arrestment in development and that the family is unable to help the child progress beyond a given point in psychological and emotional growth. Therefore, the intervention is aimed at helping the family overcome the obstacles that prevent the child from maturing in a normal, appropriate way. To achieve this goal, the team working with the patient and his family are primarily concerned with changing the rigid pattern of relationships and interpersonal transactions that hinder the normal growth processes from taking place. When the family is faced with a crisis situation, there is a good possibility that they will be receptive to opening up the family system, adopting more flexible ways of adapting to stress and beginning to deal with the crisis in a constructive manner.

The multiple impact model is designed to give help to the family during an intensive two or three day period during which the team members and family members are continuously in contact with one another, sometimes in individual interviews between a team member and a family member and sometimes in sessions during which the entire team meets with the family as a whole. The end result of the intensive work is to bring about some significant changes in the way the family perceives the problem of the adolescent presenting the problem. Recommendations as to a course of action that the family can employ to deal with the problem are set forth, and the family is asked to carry out the recommendations when they return home. The family is told that a follow-up conference will be held six months later to evaluate their progress in resolving the problems that brought on the crisis. Families are also assured that they may ask for additional consultation if the need arises before the evaluation conference is called (MacGregor, 1964).

The successful outcome of using the crisis intervention approach to helping troubled families depends on close adherence to the following principles or rules:

1. The social worker must regard crisis intervention as the treatment of choice, not a second-best approach to the family's problems.

2. Both the social worker and the family must keep in mind that there is a definite time limit and that they must proceed to resolve the problem within a relatively short period.

3. The social worker must be primarily concerned with making an accurate assessment of the immediate crisis rather than in making an extensive and thorough diagnostic evaluation.

4. Dealing with material not directly related to the crisis is to be excluded from consideration in crisis intervention.

5. The social worker must be willing to take an active and sometimes directive role in helping the family cope with the crisis.

6. The social worker relies on a flexible method of helping and gives high priority to marshaling all the resources that the family and the community can bring to aiding the family deal with stress.

Crisis intervention and its techniques require that the social worker be competent in certain basic areas.

First, helping the family to gain an intellectual understanding of the crisis by describing how a given emotionally hazardous event has produced the family crisis and disturbed the family system.

Second, helping the family members express the feelings involved in and created by the crisis situation so as to reduce tension and make it possible for the family to move on to an effective course of action for dealing with the problem.

Third, helping the family to adopt new coping methods for dealing with similar situations in the future. The last phase of crisis intervention consists of anticipatory planning whereby the social worker reinforces useful coping mechanisms and encourages the discarding of dysfunctional methods of adaptation.

Family Therapy

Helping troubled families through the use of family therapy has become an important development in social work practice. This model of helping represents a departure from the traditional casework approach in which the social worker was concerned with helping the individual in a one-to-one relationship.

Family therapy is based on the concept of the family as the unit of study and treatment. No single family member is singled out as the one person in need of help. The presence of a disturbed individual or one identified as deviant by the family is seen by the family therapist as a sign that the entire family is suffering and in need of help. The "identified patient" is the scapegoat of the disordered, dysfunctional family. The symptoms and the behavior of the individual scapegoat reflect unresolved family problems, avoided by the development of symptoms in one member. It follows that the diagnosis of the identified patient involves a careful study of the entire family system. The emphasis in family therapy shifts from a concern about what is wrong with individuals to concern with what is wrong with families. The development of family therapy represents an emphasis on the psychodynamics of the family in contrast to individually oriented approaches that emphasize the intrapsychic processes of the persons presented as patients.

This shift in emphasis from the individual to the family leads the family therapist to develop the following basic points of view:

● *Diagnosis is family centered:* A diagnosis based on the study of the individual family members does not constitute a family diagnosis. A sound basis for the practice of family therapy involves a careful examination and analysis of how the family unit functions when called upon to cope with crisis, stress or change. Therefore, the family therapist studies the individual identified as sick in the context of the family and relates the symptoms to the behavior and interaction of family members.

● *Treatment goals are family centered:* The goal of family therapy is to effect changes in the functioning of the family system. Whereas the approach in individual therapy is geared to helping the patient gain insight into the nature of his illness or his problem, family therapy is aimed at helping the family understand and alter the processes of interaction that create problems for the identified patient. In individual therapy emphasis is placed on helping the patient gain an understanding of himself as a unique person with special problems that relate only to his inner self. In family therapy the focus is on helping the family members understand themselves in relation to one another and enabling them to develop healthy forms of interaction.

● *The treatment unit is the family:* Family diagnosis focuses on the way in which family processes produce and maintain disorders in the functioning of an individual family member. The treatment process focuses on the entire family unit, rather than on the identified patient. Therefore, all members of the family are included in the therapy sessions and all are expected to contribute to the solution of the problem. In family therapy the emphasis is on the here and now, on how the therapist sees the family actually interact during interviews. The therapist and the family have an opportunity to observe how they attempt to communicate and relate to each other, how they attempt to negotiate differences, and how successful they are in resolving conflict. After the characteristic patterns of interaction have been clearly identified, the therapist is ready to move on to changing dysfunctional patterns of interaction, and helping the family develop more effective ways of communicating, negotiating and coping with conflict.

There is no one way to practice family therapy. Indeed, family therapists have found that there are several approaches to working with families, each of them having some distinguishing features while sharing the overall goal of strengthening the family unit. Among the various models of family therapy are those strongly influenced by psychoanalytic theory, those based upon communication theory, and those grounded in systems theory. Some models are oriented toward a problem-solving process and some are based on the behavioral approach to social work practice.

The work of Nathan Ackerman, a pioneer in family therapy, sees the therapist's role as that of a catalyst who stirs up family interaction, helps the members engage in exchanges of feelings and begin to relate to one another with greater depth and understanding. The therapist is intent on freeing up the sources of conflict in the family at the heart of the difficulties they face. As the therapist helps the family delve into the deeper layers of individual personal feelings, the therapist makes them aware of what lies behind the dysfunctional interaction patterns that produce neurotic or psychotic symptoms in the scapegoated family member. As each family member gets in touch with what he or she is feeling, thinking and doing, they begin to consider alternative patterns of family relationships and are able to achieve new and deeper levels of intimacy.

Like Ackerman, Murray Bowen's interest in family therapy grew out of a psychoanalytic orientation. He developed the concept of the "undifferentiated family ego mass" to explain the development of schizophrenic symptoms in a family member who could not escape a highly complicated system of interlocking symbiotic ties among family members. Bowen's goal is to help each family member achieve a sense of self by disengaging from the undifferentiated ego mass. His standard method of accomplishing this goal is to meet with two family members in order to help them take an "I" stand and break away from their habitual pattern of fusing themselves into a relationship that obstructs the normal growth and development of individual family members. Once the pathological ties are broken, each person can then achieve a greater sense of independence, autonomy and individuality (Bowen, 1978).

Virginia Satir's work in conjoint family therapy shows a strong communication theory influence, with a primary emphasis on helping the troubled family resolve problems by learning how to communicate. She often takes on the role of the teacher who helps the family understand the communication problems that she sees as the root of the troubles they face in all other aspects of their lives as a family. The role of the therapist is to be a model of communication for the family, helping the family to express feelings that have been heretofore hidden or expressed in a dysfunctional fashion. The therapeutic process consists primarily of enabling the family to develop communication skills. Once the family has acquired the skills needed to understand what each wants, the family can move on to change their interaction and open up the family system to provide opportunities for growth and personal development.

Jay Haley, one of the early researchers in family therapy, has developed a problem-solving model of therapy that requires a directive, take-charge approach by the therapist. He sees the task of the therapist as the taking of responsibility for changing the family structure and resolving the problem that brings the family into treatment. He is primarily concerned with the power alliances within the family: the way in which family members seek to maintain their position in the family system and how they maneuver to prevent change in relationships from taking place. Haley prefers using a brief, intensive form of intervention rather than long-term therapy involvement. During therapy, the family goes through a structured sequence of stages, beginning with a specific problem that the family currently faces, defining the problem in terms of how family members contribute to the problem, and suggesting ways to solve the problem. Haley makes use of assigning tasks to be carried out by the family during and between therapy sessions, with a view to getting the family to take a course of action that will be effective in solving the problem and in changing family relationships (Haley, 1976).

Salvador Minuchin (1974), whose early work involved techniques especially adapted to treating disorganized slum families from New York City, has developed several direct, concrete and action-oriented methods of intervention. His "structural therapy" is based on the view that family pathology grows out of the family's repeated reactions to stress and to rigid ways of trying to cope with stress and conflict. The object of family therapy is to break up these set patterns of reaction and replace them with functional and constructive ways of dealing with crisis and stress. In short, the family system is overloaded and disorganized. The therapist undertakes to restructure the family so that it will function more effectively. The job of the therapist is to make everyone aware that the problem they present is a family problem, rather than an individual problem, and that they must set about changing their forms of interaction. The restructuring process requires changing the rules that control the family interaction, changing the patterns of alignment among family members, and making it possible to eliminate the objectionable behaviors that cause difficulty for the family.

Robert Liberman (1970) has developed contingency contracting as a model of family therapy based upon the principles of behavior modification. A contingency contract is a means whereby family members agree to exchange mutually desired behavior. A contract is negotiated between the family members, stating what each member is to do in very explicit terms. In the process of negotiation, each participant must know exactly what he is expected to give and what he will in turn receive. The contracting is not an end in itself. It is a way of teaching the family how to communicate and express for the first time what each would like to receive and what each is willing to give. The family also experiences, often for the first time, the gratification that comes from being able to accomplish the business of implementing the contract and the ability to achieve a concrete goal. The success of contingency contracting depends on whether the family members kept their agreements and whether the contract works for the benefit of the parties involved.

Gerald Zuk, a psychologist who has developed a triadic based model of family therapy, argues that families develop faulty relationship patterns largely over issues of power and control, and that they attempt to cope with the conflict by resolving it through a third party who acts as a go between. This process results in one of the family members being scapegoated. All the problems of the family are blamed on this member who begins to accept the role, absorbs the inadequacies of the family, and develops a self-image reflecting this role. The function of the therapist is to force the family to change this pattern of using a go between process to resolve family conflict. Zuk points out that the family therapist and the family may turn out to be adversaries. The family will try to deny that anything is wrong. The therapist is challenged to show a reason for his presence. Out of this relationship between the therapist and the family the therapist may take the role of the go between who sides first with one and then a different family member. When he takes on the role of the go between, the therapist forces the family to use the process to involve one of its own members in this role. Acting in the role of go between, the therapist helps the family to negotiate and resolve conflict (Zuk, 1971).

John Bell, one of the very first to experiment with family therapy, calls his method of intervention ''family group therapy.'' Bell's purpose in therapy is to help the family become a problem-solving group that can eventually function without the therapist's help. Bell encourages the family to function very much like a team in conference, working out ways of dealing with unsatisfactory relationships among family members, working together on family problems, and reaching decisions as to how they will proceed to accomplish the goals they have set for the family. The therapist is a facilitator who helps the family determine goals and move toward them as a family unit. To achieve this objective, Bell has developed a process of moving the family through the stages of small task-oriented group development, helping the members to close gaps between them and keeping the family working together until they have attained a strong sense of unity and are able to maintain the changes that have taken place during the course of therapy (Bell, 1976).

Approaching family therapy from these various forms of practice indicates that different therapists place different emphasis on certain areas of family dysfunctioning and the intervention techniques that can be employed to bring about significant changes in family systems.

Group Approaches

Social workers have found that troubled families can be helped to cope with problems in marital relationships or difficulties in parent/ child relationships through the group process. Married couples groups are formed with the purpose of having persons with similar problems work out possible solutions through exchange of feelings, experiences, and ideas. Parenting groups are formed with a view to helping parents learn from one another and develop improved ways of handling problems of child management. In some instances, the group approach to problem-solving is the main form of intervention. In some cases it is used to supplement other forms of social work intervention.

In successive stages of working with groups, the social worker is involved in a number of different activities. During the formative stage, the worker sets about determining the purposes of the group, based upon the goals of the individual group members. Each individual has a specific purpose for joining the group. The individual's goal must be meshed with the overall purpose of the group. The worker must also establish a contract with the individual group members, setting out what obligations and responsibilities are involved in the group. The basic mechanics of operation, such as frequency of meetings, projected length of time that the group will meet, and other details are included in the early phase of group formation. The worker defines the general purpose of the group and sets the limits within which members may develop their own goals as a basis on which the group can operate.

As the group progresses, the worker assesses the effectiveness of the group process in helping individual members achieve their individual goals. Movement toward treatment objectives are expected, but the progress is not always uniform. There are periods when the group makes rapid progress, and there are also times during which the members feel that they are at an impasse and find difficulty moving ahead. The worker supports the group during periods of such difficulty and frustration, making it possible for the members to maintain a sense of cohesiveness based upon feelings of mutual trust and a desire to stay together and help each other find solutions to their individual and common problems.

Some groups are limited to a definite period of time, say eight to ten weeks. Other groups are terminated when the members and the worker conclude that the group has fulfilled its purpose; the individual members have achieved what they wanted to achieve when they joined. The worker takes responsibility for determining whether the original treatment goals for each member have been satisfied. The members themselves participate in this evaluation process, so they can perceive what they have accomplished. At the point of termination the group members are expected to transfer what they have learned to their experiences outside the group.

The use of the group approach to help parents who lack skills in parenting indicates that the group provides an opportunity for members to learn from one another. Almost all parents have some ability to demonstrate or teach other parents in the group since most of them have found that some special behavior problems of their children respond well to specific forms of interaction. The group also provides a variety of role players for model presentation and behavioral rehearsal. To demonstrate appropriate behavior, the worker can ask a group member to show other members how he has tried to solve a problem by playing the role of the parent. Other group members play the roles of other family members. The parent whose problem is being enacted is the director for the role-playing demonstration. In this capacity he instructs the other members as to how they are to perform their roles and the conditions that led to the problem with which the parent is trying to cope. The role-playing situation can be repeated several times until the parent with the problem has some confidence in working out the problem. Alternative solutions to the presented problem can be discussed by the group members and they can be asked to consider how they can apply what they have learned to their own situations.

Behavioral rehearsal is another technique found effective in helping parents learn how to perform or act in a real-life situation by rehearsing the behavior in the presence of the group. Experience has shown that this approach can be used by parents to practice such behaviors as setting limits, establishing rewards for appropriate behavior, ignoring situations that they could not previously ignore, and other areas of child management. Practicing in simulated situations makes it less difficult for the parents to perform in real life by reducing anxiety. The behavioral rehearsal usually follows some form of demonstration. After the first episode of behavioral rehearsal, other members of the group evaluate the performance and make suggestions for improvement. It is better to begin the behavioral rehearsal with situations that apply to several, if not all, the group members.

As the group progresses, the members are required to report their ability to use what they have learned to their individual problem situations. The group members monitor one another's progress in each meeting, and they develop a sense of responsibility for changing their behavior. Most parents who have participated in using behavior rehearsal feel that they are bettter able to handle their problems and better prepared to handle any new problems their children might present.

Helping couples resolve marital conflict and improve relationships has also been achieved by use of the group counseling approach. As with other groups, the worker discusses the purpose of the group, with the emphasis being placed on mutual helpfulness between group members. The group facilitator points out that each person in the group has had some life experience that could be of interest to other members faced with similar situations in their marriage. Each member therefore can benefit from this kind of exchange and gain a better understanding of their own problems. The worker makes a strong effort to make all members feel comfortable and secure in revealing their troubles and explains that what is said in the group meetings will be held in strict confidence.

Couple groups seem to be ideal for helping families resolve marital problems. Framo (1973),who has used this approach with more than 200 couples, believes it to be the most effective form of marital therapy. In the group, couples learn that the problems they face are not unique or insurmountable. Through understanding the troubles of others, members became better able to interpret their own problems and to place them in perspective. Individual members seem to find ways of applying the comments and experiences of others to solving their problems. The group experience also opens up channels of communication between partners. Although they sometimes bicker and disagree openly before the group, they at last begin to exchange suppressed feelings and ideas that had been sources of resentment for a long time. In the process of communicating, the couples usually find better ways of dealing with conflict than they used in the past. When improvements are made by a couple, other group members give them recognition for the effort put into working out their problems. The encouragement of the group leads other members to making a greater effort to achieve similar advancement in working on their problems.

Multiple Family Therapy

Multiple family therapy is an adaptation of family therapy developed by Laqueur (1971), a psychiatrist in a state hospital, who found it effective in helping a variety of dysfunctional families in which one member is undergoing treatment in the hospital. Four or five randomly selected families meet with the therapist weekly for an hour during which they share problems with one another and help each other cope with the problems of having a sick family member. The therapist acts as facilitator, guiding the discussion and keeping the families involved in the group interaction. Groups are open-ended and as one family leaves the group another family takes its place.

The benefits that families derive from this form of therapy are due to group identification and the support that they receive from one another. Special attention is given to observing the processes of communication that take place among family members. Families also learn how other families solve their problems and discover new and more effective ways of resolving conflict as a result of their participation in the group interaction. Less disturbed families are able to show other more disturbed families how to change their forms of interaction by modeling or making suggestions helpful in coping with problems.

The therapist using this model is frequently quite active in working with the group, especially in the early stages of the experience. The therapist may intervene when it is necessary to promote interaction between members of the group and to keep some families from using the time for "family visits" rather than focusing on the group's purpose. Some therapists let the group choose the subjects for discussion while others make suggestions for the group. The therapist attempts to focus attention on the basic messages that the patients and families are trying to convey. These messages are sometimes double-bind communications that leave doubt as to what is actually intended. In such cases, the therapist must cut through the peripheral material to get the family to recognize the basic meaning of what is being said. Otherwise, therapy sessions may go into unproductive digressions.

During the course of working with the group, significant developments take place. In the beginning, patients identify with other patients and families identify with other families. Within six to eight sessions, the families of the patient emerge as patients. The attitude that "they are sick and we are well" begins to break down and the longer the group continues, the less distinct the partitions between patients and family become. As the group progresses, members who have been reluctant to talk begin to open up and communicate directly with the sick family member rather than talk about him or her in front of the group. The experience provides an opportunity for patients and parents to develop new interpersonal relationships. The patient can relate to the parents of other patients because they are less threatening than his/her family members. The multiple family therapy model creates a situation in which family relationships are pooled among the group members, and it provides a wider opportunity for developing new models of behavior. The resources of all family members can be used more effectively when several families are treated together than when each family is treated as a separate entity. As Laqueur points out, "The members of a family observe what happens to other families and apply part of that knowledge to their own case. They see themselves as in a mirror in an atmosphere that is more permissive than is the case when only one family is the center of attention at all times'' (Laqueur, 1971, p. 85). Over twenty-five years, Laqueur and his colleagues have treated over 1500 families in multiple family therapy groups. Only a handful have been considered unsuited for this form of therapy, primarily because of some vital secret that could not be exposed in the group session. In the vast majority of cases, the family is able to communicate more effectively and members become able to relate to the patient in more constructive ways.

Network Intervention

A recent innovation in helping troubled families is known by the term family network intervention or retribalization. Developed by psychiatrist Ross Speck and clinical psychologist Carolyn Attneave (1973), this form of therapy attempts to mobilize the social network system to help the family resolve an emotional crisis. The intervention process includes a team of intervenors who work with the patient's relatives and the extended network of friends and relatives who can provide support for the family.

The intervention process begins with a home visit during which the team meets with the patient and his family in order to identify the problem or the crisis that needs resolution. The home visit takes about two hours and is somewhat like a mininetwork session. Family members meet and get to know the team members. After this, the team leader explains the purpose of the meeting. Each family member is encouraged to share feelings about the problem and to express opinions as to how it can be solved. Usually there is a secret or some type of painful material that the family cannot deal with openly and the team helps the family gain enough trust and confidence to explore the nature of this underlying source of difficulty. Team members and family then determine whether the family needs the help of other persons who could be helpful. When a decision has been reached to attempt networking intervention, the family is asked to prepare a list of family and friends to be involved in the networking process. The group to be invited are given a brief statement of the problem and the family's need to have help in solving it. The network consists of forty or more persons who meet in the home of the patient for about two days for a total of six to eight hours.

According to Speck and Attneave, family network intervention usually proceeds through six distinct phases, including retribalization, polarization, mobilization, depression, breakthrough and exhaustion/elation. The initial *retribalization* phase occurs when the network first assembles and the people who have been invited become acquainted with new people and reconnect with family members whom they may not have seen for a long time. The team facilitates the retribalization process and increases the involvement of the network by encouraging the members to mill around the room, followed by activities that allow them to express physical energy such as jumping up and down, clapping hands and singing. The team leader explains why the meeting has been called and sets out the goals of the networking process. For many in the network, this is the first time that they are aware that the family has a serious problem. The immediate family members are seated in a place in the center of the room and outline what they think about the problem and what help they expect to receive from the network.

The *polarization* phase follows this retribalization phase. During polarization, the network participants contribute their views about the problem and how the family crisis should be resolved. As the network enters this phase, certain members become the "activists," the individuals who initiate collaborative efforts to solve the problem. The intervention team facilitates the process by encouraging small groups to form and discuss possible alternative solutions. As the problem is defined, various members more or less consciously choose up sides.

The polarization phase is followed by the *mobilization* phase during which the team encourages the members to consider what tasks need to be undertaken to solve the crisis. At this point the group will feel somewhat discouraged by their inability to find a quick solution to the problem. This is the *depression* phase that results when the members feel that their suggestions are rejected by the group and they realize that the resolution of the crisis will take longer than they anticipated. The team helps the group acknowledge that they are "stuck" and helps the members renew their efforts to help the family. This is the *breakthrough* phase that is characterized by increased activity and optimism. The group begins to feel that there are workable solutions to the problem and that the efforts will finally pay off.

During the breakthrough phase, the team members help the group form support groups that will contribute some specific help to the family and will carry out some special responsibility or task after the network meeting has ended. These support groups are usually composed of the group members who have been most active and are willing to help the family carry out some concrete action such as finding a job, offering financial help, or making alternative living arrangements. The support groups are temporary, remaining active for about three weeks to three months after the network process has been started.

The goal that underlies the networking process is to stimulate, reflect and focus the potential of the family network to solve problems. "There is no single goal — not cure, not treatment — but enabling people to cope and to share their strengths in coping and also reap enjoyments and pleasures that restore their potentials and set them up to handle the inevitable next crisis of living," write Speck and Attneave (1973, p. 50). If the intervenors are clear about this goal, they will keep in mind the need to refrain from providing solutions themselves and will continue to give the responsibility for solving the problem to the family network. The skills that the intervention team needs to accomplish the goals of networking include: the ability to relate to people, to sense group moods and group strengths, to facilitate, to reflect back confidence in the capacity of the group to develop creative solutions during the course of therapy.

Using network intervention and family support systems seems to be effective in a wide variety of dysfunctional types of situations, particularly with family disorganization associated with suicide attempts, depression that results from family break-up, separation and divorce, and psychotic behavior patterns. The selection of families for network intervention is based on the following criteria: the nature and scope of the problem, the degree of the family's desperation, previous efforts made to deal with the problem, the availability of enough people to form a network and the willingness of the family to call upon friends and relatives to resolve the crisis. Network intervention has been found to be especially effective with family situations not resolved by other forms of therapy. The more desperate the members of the family are to find solutions, the better are the chances that networking will succeed. The willingness of the family to assemble the network is of vital importance. Some families find the process too difficult. They would rather deal with the problem without public exposure; the sharing of painful feelings with others is too much for them to face. These feelings must be respected, and the final decision left to family members. However, as Speck and Attneave point out, "The prospects of institutionalization, unending entrapment or physical danger to oneself or a loved one seem far more threatening than the public nature of network assembly, especially if there is hope that the intervention will lay to rest the ghosts for the future" (1973, p. 41).

References

Ackerman, N. W. *Treating the troubled family*. New York: Basic Books, 1966.

Bell, J. E. *Family therapy*. New York: Jason Aronson, 1975.

Bowen, M. *Family therapy in clinical practice*. New York: Jason, Aronson, 1978.

Framo, J. L. Marriage therapy in a couples group. In D. A. Bloch (Ed.), *Techniques of family therapy: A Primer*. New York: Grune and Stratton, 1973.

Haley, J. *Problem solving therapy*. San Francisco: Jossey-Bass, 1976.

Hawkins, R. P. et al. Behavior therapy in the home. In J. Haley (Ed.), *Changing families*. New York: Grune and Stratton, 1971.

Laqueur, H. P. et al. Multiple family therapy; further developments. In J. Haley (Ed.), *Changing families*. New York: Grune and Stratton, 1971.

Liberman, R. P. Behavioral approaches to family and group therapy. *American Journal of Orthopsychiatry*, 1970, *40*, 106-118.

MacGregor, R. et al. *Multiple impact therapy with families*. New York: McGraw-Hill, 1964.

Minuchin, S. *Families and family therapy*. Cambridge, Mass.: Harvard University Press, 1974.

Pittman, F. S. et al. Therapy techniques of the family unit. In J. Haley (Ed.), *Changing families*. New York: Grune and Stratton, 1971.

Satir, V. *Conjoint family therapy*. Palo Alto, Calif.: Science and Behavior Books, 1967.

Speck, R. & Attneave, C. L. *Family networks*. New York: Pantheon Books, 1973.

Zuk, G. *Family therapy: A triadic-based approach*. New York: Human Sciences Press, 1971.

FOUR

Solving Family Problems

Although each family's problems are unique in some important respect, the difficulties most families confront fall into one or more of four major catagories: 1) problems in the relationship between husband and wife; 2) problems in the relationship of parents to children; 3) personal adjustment problems of a child or adult member of the family; or 4) problems related to an environmental situation that is a source of stress on the family.

These categories are not mutually exclusive. A given family may have problems in interpersonal relationships and also face difficulties in coping with its environment. Indeed, the latter two types of problems may be related in an important causal and interactional fashion. The environmental situation may cause or aggravate a difficulty in the relationship between husband and wife or parents and children. In turn, the family's difficulty in solving problems of interpersonal relationships can adversely affect the ability to cope with the stress that comes from the environment.

Moreover, the personal adjustment of a family member may be the result of some difficulty in the relationship between family members. A child may develop a behavior disorder or an adult may show symptoms of a personality disorder when family relationships become disturbed or chaotic. In turn, the disorder or problem of the individual family member may result in a further breakdown in the family system.

Therefore, the family sometimes presents more than one type of problem, in many cases intertwined in a complex pattern of interac-

tion between family members and the family's environment. The
helping process becomes correspondingly complicated. Not all problems can be dealt with simultaneously. Therefore, attention is focused
on one specific area of dysfunctioning in each stage of the intervention
by the social worker. The overall purpose of the work with the family
is to help family members develop and improve problem-solving
skills that can be used by the family to solve problems in interpersonal relationships, problems of personal adjustment, or problems
created by the environment.

Resolving Marital Problems

Problems between husband and wife constitute the major source of
difficulty for troubled families, according to a nationwide survey
conducted by the Family Service Association of America (Beck,
1973). The survey inquired into the various aspects of the marital
relationship that were a source of concern for the clients who sought
help. Communication problems were found to be the area in which
most families had difficulty. Almost nine out of ten couples who
presented marital problems were facing serious difficulties communicating with one another. As clients put it: "We can't talk to each
other"; "I can't seem to reach him"; or "Every time we try to
talk to each other it leads to an argument."

Conflicts about children's problems were found to be another area
of difficulty for marital couples. They often reported that they could
not agree on how to handle disciplinary problems and did not share
the same views about child-rearing practices. Sexual difficulties
were reported almost as frequently as child-related problems and
involved more than four out of ten couples who sought help. Conflicts over money and leisure time activities were reported by about
one couple in three; infidelity in one couple out of four. Other
sources of conflict were found to involve relationships to in-laws,
housekeeping standards, and physical abuse or assault.

These findings indicate that helping couples resolve marital problems must necessarily focus on the communication difficulties the
partners are experiencing. If they cannot communicate feelings and
thoughts clearly and honestly, there is little possiblity that they can
find a way of resolving their conflicts. Social workers therefore put
considerable effort into helping couples overcome obstacles to
communication, showing them how to develop new patterns of interaction in giving and receiving messages.

Social workers also focus on helping the couple improve their
negotiating skills. Emphasis is placed on the use of "marital bar-

gaining,'' a process whereby both partners stand to gain something important to them. The pattern of dominance and submission that usually causes problems is gradually modified and the partners establish a relationship based upon equality and mutual respect for the right to be heard. The social worker's role in helping the partners learn to negotiate is illustrated in the following case.

David was recently graduated from a state university with a degree in computer science. His wife, Anna, had gone to work in an insurance agency so that David could complete his schooling. She took major responsibility for providing economic support for the family, including a two year old son. Eventually Anna received several promotions. Each promotion brought her to realize that she was now really developing unusual skills as an administrative assistant to the vice-president of a large corporation. Her work had become a source of great pride and satisfaction.

Meanwhile, David had been struggling to find employment as a computer analyst. The first year, he had gained enough experience to consider increased responsibilities in his chosen field, but the firm employing him could not provide him a chance to move up to the better position he felt he was qualified for. David began to look elsewhere for a better paying job, and was interviewed for a position with a firm located in another city.

Anna first made no protest when David announced that he wanted to accept the job and relocate. David began to notice that Anna was gradually becoming irritable and withdrawn. She had been quite responsive in love-making. Anna now tried to avoid sex. She began to find fault with David over trivial matters that had not troubled her before. In turn David began to retreat, drank more than usual, and accused Anna of being frigid. At this point, he suggested they seek the professional help of a social worker recommended by a friend. Anna agreed.

In the first session, the social worker encouraged David and Anna to express their feelings. Anna said she realized that she had been withdrawing from David. With the social worker's help, she identified the events which had led to their inability to bridge the emotional distance which had begun to widen in the past two weeks. While she had seemingly agreed to David's plan to accept the new job in another city, Anna had not actually wanted to make the move. Why had she agreed? First, because it meant a better job for David. Second, because she thought David would be angry if she objected.

In this initial session, David listened attentively while Anna talked about her feelings. She told him that he had not taken into account her own job as an important consideration. She had worked hard to get to a position where her abilities had been recognized. Now she would have to give up her well earned positon and begin over again. She also expressed anger toward David, pointing out that she had worked hard to support the family so he could complete his education. Her resentment exploded and she ended the session in tears.

In the second session, David was asked to describe how he had reacted to Anna's anger and tears. He said he did not really know what he felt. He did acknowledge that Anna had helped him through school, but he had always thought that her work was only a temporary stop-gap measure. He had not realized that her work had become so important to her. It apparently meant more to her than he had realized. In fact, he had even thought that she would be glad to quit work, stay home, and be a full-time mother and wife. Now that he had an opportunity for a good-paying job, the family would no longer need to depend upon Anna's income.

The social worker suggested that the problem was actually a failure in communication. Anna had not revealed her feelings of anger and resentment openly so that David would understand the reasons for her withdrawal and irritability. David, in turn, had seen Anna's reaction to the move as irrational, stubborn, and frustrating. Now that they had finally brought the matter out into the open, the social worker suggested that they begin to come to an agreement satisfactory to both of them.

The social worker directed the negotiating process by asking Anna to propose a solution that she thought would be acceptable to David. She again told David that she thought she was not being treated fairly. She would have to give up a job which meant much more to her than a paycheck. David said he now realized how important the job was, but he also had to consider his own future.

In the following session the social worker asked David to put forth a solution to the problem in changing jobs. David suggested that Anna might find a job where they moved. He would not expect her to give up the idea of working. Would she be willing to explore job possibilities in Dallas, where his job was located?

Anna was willing to agree, but only if it did not mean taking a job far below her present level. If there were opportunities for her in Dallas, she would feel that the move would really work out. The social worker suggested they exchange their views over the weekend at home.

In the following session, the social worker asked each to determine their individual responsibility to carry out the agreement. David said he would not make a decision until Anna had an opportunity to explore job possibilities. He would arrange to go with her, if she wanted him to. Anna expressed her appreciation. She said she would make some preliminary inquiries about jobs and set up some appointments for interviews. David took responsibility for making plans for their trip. Both said they could arrange to take time off from work to investigate job possibilities. Anna's reaction was quite positive. "Hey, it's really exciting! Maybe I'll find a job that is even better than the one I have." They agreed to return and report their progress.

The steps which the social worker took in helping the couple in this case involved a clarification of how the change in jobs had become a problem for both David and Anna. Once this problem had been identified as a failure in communication, the helping process was directed to opening up the channels of communication so that each could express and exchange suppressed feelings. The mutual sharing of feelings laid the groundwork for negotiation of a solution to the problem.

Sexual relationships are frequently a source of difficulty in many marriages. The problem usually involves some dissatisfaction in a particular aspect of sexual functioning such as lack of interest or desire, inadequacy in achieving orgasm, or differences over the frequency and timing of sexual relations.

The less complicated difficulties in sexual response may respond to an educational approach. Some couples do not have adequate or correct information about sexual functioning. Young couples may come into marriage with little or no sex education. Middle-age couples may feel that their sexual life is not as fulfilling or exciting as it once was. Older couples may not understand the natural changes in sex needs that occur in later life. In such many cases, providing the couple with relevant and accurate information can bring about change and raise the level of sexual response significantly. A case in point is the following.

Mr. and Mrs. C. consulted a marriage counselor to discuss their sexual problems. They had been quite happily married for five years. However, Mrs. C. said she had never experienced a "natural climax." She confided that only when her husband stimulated her clitoris in masturbation could she achieve orgasm. Both partners thought this practice abnormal. The couple also said that Mrs. C. enjoyed sex when she assumed the superior, on top, position, but she was hesitant to express her wishes to Mr. C. for fear he might consider her an overly aggressive dominating woman. A simple straightforward explanation that most women required stimulation of the clitoris and assurance that a wide variety of positions enhanced sexual pleasure was all that was needed to help the couple achieve a satisfactory sexual adjustment.

In some cases the social worker may find that the sexual difficulty grows out of serious problems in other areas of relationship. The sexual problem is not the basic cause of marital dissatisfaction. Improvement in the sexual relations will come about once the other problems in the marriage are satisfactorily resolved. An example is the case of Mr. and Mrs. J.

Mr. and Mrs. J. had been married ten years when Mrs. J. had told her husband she wanted a divorce. She explained that she had not enjoyed sex during the past year and that her husband's demands for sexual relations had become intolerable. Mr. J. admitted that their sexual life had been a problem, and he had been hurt by his wife's refusal to have sex.

A study of the history of the sexual difficulty showed that Mrs. J.'s disinterest in sex occurred soon after Mr. J. had been promoted to a more responsible job as plant foreman. She noticed an abrupt change in her husband. Before his promotion Mr. J. had been a "good husband," and the couple agreed that their sex life had been very satisfying. Only recently had Mr. J. become extremely irritable around his wife and children. There were frequent quarrels and on several occasions Mr. J. had threatened to strike his wife.

Mrs. J. acknowledged that she had withdrawn from her husband and that her affection for him had been seriously undermined by his behavior. She resented his abusive language and his threats of violence. Her hostility had reached the point where she could no longer respond to him sexually.

Marriage counselors can often help couples realize that sex is not the only problem in their marital relationship. Once they see that the sexual difficulties are part of a total relationship, they can begin to work toward solving their marital problems. As they find solutions to their marital problems, the sexual adjustment usually improves without intensive or prolonged sex therapy.

In assessing problems of sexual adjustment, the marriage counselor can gain understanding of the couple's difficulties by asking these questions: What attracts the partners sexually? How do they like to have sex initiated? What do they consider the appropriate role for the man and the woman in sex? How frequently do they want sex? What gives them sexual pleasure or enhances their sexual enjoyment? Are other persons to be included in their sex relations, or is sex to be the exclusive right of the husband or wife?

The physical appearance of their mate is important to most people. Special features may be the center of sexual attraction — breasts, buttocks, legs, eyes, hair, facial expression. Physique, height and body build may also be significant sources of sexual attraction. Provocative clothing is generally sexually stimulating, as is the use of perfumes and scents. Other features include tone of voice, use of gestures, and other symbolic expressions of seduction. Sources of sexual attraction are idiosyncratic, with a wide range of preference for physical features among both males and females. A knowledge of what attracts and what repels is fundamental to the partners' ability to maintain a maximum degree of sexuality in the relationship. If each knows what ''turns on'' the other and what ''turns off'' the partner, the relationship takes on additional sexual excitement.

Partners often feel that one or the other must always initiate sex by a sign of sexual interest. Couples usually develop a subtle kind of communication or ritual which precedes intercourse and is used to indicate sexual desire. In some marriages, both partners hesitate to signal a desire for sex because they fear rejection. Since it is too painful to risk rejection, neither takes the initiative. If both partners can accept the fact that they can give pleasure to their mate even though they themselves are not sexually aroused, most difficulties can be overcome. The wife may offer to give her husband sexual pleasure even though she does not want to be sexually excited. There are other times when the husband can accept the wife's desire for sexual intercourse although he may not have initiated sexual activity. The ideal situation is one in which both partners feel free to initiate sex without feeling guilty or fearing rejection.

Sexual stereotypes can be strong barriers to full sexual enjoyment. Preconceived notions as to what is appropriate sexual conduct for a woman or a man are difficult to overcome. Women who may want to be open and spontaneous in the sexual act may inhibit their sexual drives if they have been taught that such behavior is ''wanton'' and that her partner will take offense if she shows an active interest in certain forms of behavior such as oral sex or certain positions in coitus. Unlearning preconceived ideas inculcated in either partner may play an important role in helping them achieve a more rewarding and satisfying sexual experience. Therefore, it is wise to explore the feelings about sexual roles in assessing the sexual relationship. Must the man always initiate sexual activity? Is the man on top the only position to be used? Are sex roles rigidly defined, or are they flexible?

Communication of sex needs is essential if the couple is to overcome obstacles to sexual fulfillment. Each needs to let the other know what gives pleasure and what is sexually exciting. The desire for some variation in the sexual act is quite normal. Exploring new ways of creating sexual desire and finding a variety of pleasureable sex outlets will enhance and maintain a high level of sexual activity and interest. This might include the use of sexual talk between them or the use of fantasy — either spoken or non-verbal — which can be employed to heighten sexual interest. Mild sadomasochistic play, callgirl fantasies, or troilism fantasies are stimulating sexual devices for some persons. Others may use physical aids such as body oils, vibrators, or the wearing of certain clothing as sexual stimulants to enhance pleasure. If both partners are willing to use some imagination, they may find ways of adding excitement to their sex life.

Including another person in the couple's sex relationship, as in troilism, may sometimes be used to add excitement to the sexual activity. For many couples the fantasy is more exciting than the reality. While some find group sex adds to their sexual interest in the marriage partner, others find that such activities as mate-swapping or group sex are disruptive to their marriage relationship and give it up after a brief period of experimentation.

In the role of marriage counselor, the social worker can help the couple negotiate the terms of their sexual contracts, just as they might negotiate contracts which cover other aspects of their marriage, such as income management or child-rearing. The contract should cover the areas of sexual activity outlined above, and each partner should be prepared to say what he or she will give and what he or she expects in return. The following is an example of how a couple can negotiate a sexual contract.

Mr. and Mrs. N. had been married three years. During the first two years, they had consistently engaged in sexual intercourse four or five times per week. In the past year, their interest in sex had declined, and intercourse was limited to occasional sex on weekends.

A preliminary exploration of the couple's sexual functioning indicated that both were free of any serious psychological or physical dysfunctions which could account for the decline in their sexual relationship. Mechanically, sex was good for both of them, and intercourse usually ended in orgasm for both partners. But sex was not emotionally satisfying to the wife. She felt distance between herself and her husband in the sexual act. As she expressed it, "I just don't feel that he loves me, even though technically he is a very good lover."

A more detailed inquiry into the sex relations showed that Mrs. N. felt that her husband withdrew from her both physically and emotionally once they had reached orgasm. She wanted sex to end with a strong feeling of being loved and cared for by her husband. His turning away from her after sex had been completed was an indication to her that he was rejecting her emotionally. As the feeling of rejection and abandonment surfaced, Mrs. N. began to enjoy sex less, and was beginning to fear that she was losing her ability to achieve orgasm.

Mr. N. had noticed that his wife was showing some signs of depression. He had accounted for the decline in their sex life to her emotional state, thinking that perhaps there were also some physical reasons for her lack of sexual desire. When he had tried to discuss the matter of her health, Mrs. N. brushed the question aside, and eventually he accepted her refusal to talk about the problem.

Mrs. N. said she had not told him about her feelings of being unloved and her fear of being abandoned because it would make her vulnerable. She thought that Mr. N. would regard her desire for a display of affection in intercourse as childish and romantic, something that might amuse or irritate him.

To restore the sexual functioning to the previous level of satisfaction, the couple negotiated a new sexual contract. Mrs. N. agreed to tell Mr. N. whenever she became depressed or anxious because of her need for affection. Mr. N. in turn agreed to listen to her expressions and feelings of insecurity without discounting the importance of what she was telling him. In turn, Mrs. N. agreed to resume the role of an adequate sex partner, and now felt that she could give herself freely to her husband in sex without feeling anxious and insecure.

The success in negotiating a satisfactory sexual contract rests upon the ability of the two partners to be open and honest in their communication. As in other areas of marital discord, the resolution of the difficulty can be resolved if the problem can be clearly identified and accurately assessed. When this stage has been reached, the social worker can set in motion a plan of intervention which will help the couple achieve the desired outcome of treatment.

Helping Separated Persons

Even the best efforts of social worker and client may not resolve the conflict. A separation or divorce may seem to be the solution. In such cases, the responsibility for making the decision to end a marriage must be the responsibility of the couple, without the social worker's bias for or against separation influencing the final outcome. Even though the social worker has strong opinions as to the wisdom of a particular course of action, the client's right to self-determination and decision-making takes precedence over the counselor's feelings.

The process of marital separation often presents serious emotional and practical problems for one or both marital partners. Even though the marriage has been filled with conflict and hurt, the separation experience is usually a period of intense emotional upheaval. The emotional reactions following separation vary. In some cases a depression follows soon after the separation and persists for several months. The social worker can help the individual through the depression in most cases by offering emotional support and guiding the client through feelings of loss of an attachment which has played an important part in his or her life.

Once the separation has become a reality, the partners have a need to develop new identities. The separation brings about an initial feeling that the old self no longer exists and and a new self has not yet emerged. The familiar world around may appear strange and even frightening. Eventually the confusion begins to disappear and the individual will develop a new coherent self. But the formation of a new identity is a slow process, and for a time the separated person may feel that his/her life is without direction.

The absence of a sense of identity makes planning for the future difficult. Separated persons may vacillate, deciding first on one course of action and then another. Others put off making decisions, while still others may act impulsively upon suggestions of others without carefully weighing the consequences of the decision. Ill-advised changes in jobs, moving from one house to another, or other abrupt changes may later prove to more disruptive than helpful. The social worker may be of great assistance in helping the separated person through this state of confusion and indecision. Through sympathetic understanding during this difficult stage social workers may help the client avoid decisions based upon impulsive emotional reactions rather than on a rational appraisal of the alternative courses of action.

As Weiss points out, many separated persons become involved in "obsessive review" of the past (1975, p. 247). The separated individual becomes extremely preoccupied with such questions as, "Why didn't I try harder to make the marriage work?'' or ''What could I have done that would have make things turn out differently?'' Some persons wonder if they made a wise decision. Others review all the humiliation and hurt they underwent during the marriage, only to have it finally end in divorce. While obsessive review may make the acceptance of the reality of divorce somewhat less painful, it can also lead to a serious problem. Inability to concentrate can interfere with the individual's capacity to function and carry out other survival tasks. Obsessive review can also cause the separated person to become so hopelessly entangled in the past that s/he is unable to make decisions about the future.

The social worker can help the separated person through the obsessive review phase in several ways. While the passage of time is always an important healing factor, those unable to escape the past can use professional help to bring themselves into the present. The social worker can also help the client distinguish between reality and fantasy about the past. S/he can relieve unwarranted guilt reactions when someone wrongly takes the blame for the failure of the marriage. As the separated person begins to regard the parting in a more realistic perspective, s/he can regain confidence in an ability to function normally and focus energies on the future.

In addition to these emotional hazards, separated people also face a number of practical problems. Support payments for the children are usually not adequate and must be supplemented by the mother's earnings. The separated woman may have been out of the labor market for a considerable period of time. Her confidence in her ability to find employment may be at a low ebb. Even the thought of competing for a job may cause her to become extremely anxious. In other cases, the separated or divorced woman may have no marketable skills to offer and will need to consider special training or additional education. The social worker can usually assist the separated woman equip herself for employment by referring her to resources that will assess her abilities and provide any needed training. Some women are quite capable of solving these practical problems without help or counseling, but many need the psychological support the social worker can supply, as well as the information and guidance which the counselor can make available.

In some situations, the social worker takes the role of advocate for the separated person. While most separated persons have sufficient funds to employ an attorney to represent them, it may be difficult for the poor to obtain a divorce without free legal service. Social workers can help clients obtain competent legal services when legal-aid offices show a reluctance to accept divorce cases because of more urgent matters.

The poor also need public assistance to provide for basic family necessities. Application for public welfare can be a difficult and sometimes a humiliating experience. In some cases, the welfare department may require that the applicant mother bring legal action for support in a court of law. Support orders can be made, but among poor families, the money is seldom forthcoming. Even middle-class families find that there are recurring legal battles over failure to provide support. The social worker in cooperation with a competent and interested attorney can protect the right of the mother to adequate support from the father or the right to public assistance.

The help social workers can offer separated persons on an individual basis can be augmented by group counseling. Group therapy and group counseling have proven to be effective in helping clients cope with a wide variety of problems, including drug addiction, child abuse, and mental illness. The group experience can also serve a useful purpose for separated persons. The separated person can receive help through the support and understanding of group members facing similar problems in making the transition from being married to being separated.

Seminars for the separated have been developed under the leadership of Dr. Robert S. Weiss at Harvard University (1975, pp. 311-317). Their purpose has been to help recently separated individuals manage the social and emotional impact of divorce. The seminar consists of eight weekly sessions. Each session deals with a specific topic, such as the emotional impact of separation, the continuing relationship with ex-husband and wife, and reactions of friends and kin to the separation. Other topics included in the seminar deal with change in parents' relationship to children and how parents can help their children cope with the absence of a father or mother. Separated persons are also helped to build a new life, and establish a new identity.

The seminars provide an opportunity for small group discusson under the guidance of a qualified group leader. The leader acts as a facilitator, encouraging the group members to respond to one another. Information from others assures the participants that they are not alone and that others also find marital separation a trying experience. The group members also begin to find that their problems are manageable, and that others are working out solutions and putting their lives back together again.

Does divorce have long-lasting psychological effects on children? Evidence obtained from studies of children of divorced parents indicates that they do not all suffer disabilities or that they are more likely to have emotional problems than children whose parents do not divorce (Weiss, 1975, p. 213). Although parental separation often temporarily disturbs the client's feeling of security, a stable parent can help the child survive without suffering permanent damage.

Children's reactions to separation vary. According to a clinical study conducted by Judith S. Wallerstein and Joan B. Kelly, most children are upset at first by the separation, irrespective of age (Weiss, 1975, p. 213). The great majority of preadolescent children are usually saddened by the separation and will regress to earlier ways of functioning, have problems in sleeping, or will develop somatic symptoms such as cramps or asthma. Some have temper tantrums, others develop fantasies. Young children sometimes blame themselves for the separation.

Some adolescents may be angry at their parents because they think parental separation is a disgrace. Some adolescents idealize the parent who has left the family and blame the remaining parent for the divorce. Adolescents frequently express resentment if the parent begins to date. Children sometimes set out on well planned programs to prevent remarriage or try to prevent the parent from becoming involved with someone new.

Research studies of divorced families provide some general principles that social workers can use in working with parents and children in divorced or separated families that can be summarized as follows:

- Children of all ages should be told the truth about the separation. Otherwise, they will have to make their own interpretation, and their interpretation of the separation will probably be inaccurate.
- Children are apt to be upset by the separation and need the parents' understanding. Therefore, the parent will need to give more time and attention to the children than s/he ordinarily would.
- Children who fail to resume normal development within a year of the separation may need special attention. In such cases the parent should be urged to seek the help of a competent child therapist.
- A competent and self-confident parent is the child's most important source of security. Children whose mothers are able to cope with the problems of separation themselves and who reestablish an identity are likely to help their children survive without permanent damage.
- Ordinarily, it is wise for the noncustody parent, usually the father, to remain in the picture. The father can continue to play an important role in the child's life even though he is no longer a member of the household.

- Abrupt changes in living situations should be avoided if possible. The child who continues to live in familiar surroundings, attend the same school, and retain his established friendships is apt to suffer minimum damage from the break-up of the marriage.
- Children should be allowed to mature at their own pace. Parents may be tempted to become overly protective and seek to keep children from maturating by trying to protect them from any source of anxiety or frustration. Some parents may expect their children to become responsible in ways beyond their ability or to become confidants, companions, and advisors. Either extreme should be avoided.
- The parent need not become a martyr. Children need a parent's help, but when the parent sacrifices his/her own best interest to the child's, the consequences are usually disastrous for both.

Social workers can be of great help in making the transition from marriage to divorce less painful for both the parents and the children. Working with both the adults and the children is essential in most cases because the ripple effect presents all involved with special problems that must be solved.

Changing Parent/Child Relations

The relationship between children and parents is a source of difficulty for many families, ranking second among the concerns reported by families who sought the help of family social workers (Beck, 1973). As the family expands with the arrival of children, new problems in relationships develop and the family reacts to the changes that take place in the family system. The social worker can play an important role in helping the family make a satisfactory adjustment to these changes.

One of the most troublesome periods in family life comes when the children enter adolescence. Parents have difficulty coping with teenagers' unstable emotional states, and are also concerned when adolescent children begin to challenge their parents' traditional values and life style. Generational gaps create problems as the young adult begins to make more demands for freedom from parental authority, independence in making decisions, and a larger measure of personal autonomy.

The social worker's efforts to help the family develop new directions as the life cycle changes are important. The social worker may help the family achieve competence in solving relationship problems by focusing attention on communication between parents and children, helping the family develop effective ways of negotiating, and resolving conflicts as illustrated in the following case.

The therapist is a social worker on the staff of a family service agency. He has asked all family members to meet with him to discuss the problem of the sixteen year old son, Harold, who was taken into police custody. The social worker begins to explore the problem with the family. They report that Harold was found sleeping in the local bus station at 2 A.M., and a police officer brought him home. Harold told the police that he had had a dispute with his stepfather, who ordered him to leave the house and not come back. Mr. Simmons, Harold's stepfather, admitted that he had lost his temper but that he was desperate and did not know what else to do. Tension between Mr. Simmons and Harold had become serious, according to Harold's mother. She did not blame her husband for being upset, but she told the social worker that he was wrong in ordering Harold to leave the house. She said she had hoped, ''Things could be worked out and we could all get along with each other and stop this terrible fighting.'' Mr. Simmons said something had to be done, but he did not know what.

The social worker explained that he wanted to discuss the problem with the entire family, and that he was interested in finding out what each member of the family thought needed to be changed if things were to improve and the conflict between Harold and his parents resolved. The social worker first turned to the father and invited him to express his point of view. The following verbatim excerpts from the first family session indicate how the social worker engaged the family in a discussion of the problems that have been troubling them.

Father: Well, I'm not home a lot. I'm out on the road most of the time. And when I come home, I expect to have some peace and quiet. I can't stand all this fighting. I want all this fighting stopped — between Eddie and his mother and Eddie and his sister. I come home and I'm tired. Things were never like this in my home.

Therapist: Are these quarrels that break out?

Father: Yes, all the quarreling, arguing, yelling.

Mother: But that's not so easy you know.

Therapist: What isn't easy?

Mother: Okay. I'm tired. I have to fix supper. I'm trying to do that. And then there is all this trouble between them. You know? I'm trying, but get tired and I can't. . . .

Father: If they are going to fight, then do it when I'm not there. That's all I ask.

Therapist: You want the fighting to stop. Anything else you want to see changed?

Father: I think Eddie has to make some concessions. I've tried to do things for him. I try to bring home things he would like. And I've tried to get him interested in Little League. I try to spend some time with him. I've really tried to get along with him, but he has to meet me halfway, at least I'd like for him to.

Therapist: I get the feeling maybe you and Eddie don't like each other. Or what is it? What's going on between you two?

Father: Yeah. I think there is some resentment there. You know I'm his stepfather, not his real father. Could make a difference. Maybe that's it.

Mother: I think I ought to tell you about that. Eddie has said something on different occasions about living with his real father. And I told him, it just can't be. Well, anyway, he keeps on with all this, and I don't know what the answer is. And he won't listen to me. I can't control him. There are always fights going on. Things are getting real bad. And so that's why we are here. We went to another place. That didn't help. That was four year ago, and I thought then maybe . . .

Therapist: Look, I would like to go back to what Dad said, and see if I understand. Dad, I want to ask you something.

Father: Yeah. Okay.

Therapist: You want to get on better terms with Eddie, or do you want him to leave. What do you think?

Father: Well no, I don't really want him to leave, not if he can get along with his sister and his mother.

Therapist: I'm interested in this, Ken. Do you think there is a good chance that things could work out better? Is there a fifty-fifty chance?

Father: I don't really know. Things have been pretty bad the last two months.

Therapist: And that bothers you?

Father: Yes, it does. Very much.

Therapist: Cause some trouble between you and Bonita?

Father: Very much so.

Therapist: Well, let's see what Mom has to say. *(To mother)* What would you like to see changed? What would you like to see happen in your family?

Mother: I'd like for us to be a happy family. And I'd like for Eddie to act better.

Therapist: Well, now could you make that a little more clear for me. What would make your family happy?

Mother: Well, if we got along better, and if we could be happy, like we should be.

Father: I think she wants all the yelling and fighting to stop.

Eddie: You want to get rid of me. *(Looks toward mother)*

Mother: No, I didn't say....

Eddie: Yes you did. You *both* did.

Therapist: You know, I'm getting a little confused. A while ago I thought Mom was asking for someone in this family to help her.

Mother: Well, I'm pretty exhausted with all this fighting, arguing and yelling. All the trouble. I don't know what I'm supposed to do. Or what I can do anymore. Ken was doing everything he could at one time, but then....

Therapist: You want to say something, Ken?

Father: I think that maybe if Eddie realized that we want him and if he would relate to us in some way or some sense that we want him.

Therapist: So, you think that if Eddie really felt that you want him, you think that would change things for the better?

Father: Right, he calls everybody names, he fights with everybody, he has these tantrums, you know.

Therapist: I understand that. But what I want to know is whether you think that if Eddie would feel more accepted and wanted that would....

Mother: Yeah, I think if he realized that we love him then that would help him to ah....

(The family begins the session by a recital of how Eddie disrupts the family. Then the father begins to examine his relationship to Eddie, defining the problem as an uncomfortable or unhappy relation to Eddie that needs to be resolved. The father enlarges on this point, remarking that perhaps the problem could be solved if Eddie felt that the family loved him. The therapist next explores Eddie's view of the problem.)

Therapist: Eddie what do you want changed?

Eddie: I want to go live with my *real* father. Mom got rid of him. I like him. We got along okay. They tried to send me away. *(Looking at mother and step-father.)* To some kind of school.

Therapist: Mom and Ken think that maybe you don't feel like you're wanted in this family, that you are not welcome.

What if Ken wanted you to stay? Mom wanted you to stay? I don't know about Chris [the sister].

Eddie: It would be okay if everybody just quit yelling at me about everything. Just everything around the house.

Therapist: Who yells?

Eddie: Mom, Dad, Chris. They don't yell at Chris. They always yell at me.

Therapist: What do they yell at you about?

Eddie: Fighting with Chris. But they never find anything wrong with her. Just me. Chris yells. Then Mom yells at me. Then Dad yells at me.

Therapist: Sounds like you're the bad guy in this family. What about Chris? Maybe she's the trouble-maker?

Eddie: Like I say, she never gets yelled at.

The dialogue between the therapist and Eddie confirms that he is the identified patient, the cause of the family's difficulties. The therapist comments to the family: "Sounds like if Eddie would just shape up and do right there would be no problems in your family." This statement is not acceptable to the family now, at least not in its full implications. There is an indication that the family feels some responsibility for what is happening to Eddie. Even the six year old daughter admits, "Sometimes they are really not too fair. I get by with more things because I'm little."

In helping the family define the problem, the therapist is careful to enlist the participation of all family members, and to make sure that family members are aware of what each is trying to communicate. In most cases, a structured initial interview provides some safeguards to prevent one family member from dominating the session and giving the other family members little opportunity to define the problem from their point of view. If the therapist is careful to enlist the input of all members, the family comes away with a feeling that he is not taking sides, but is interested in finding out what is happening and what the family members think might be possible solutions to their difficulties. The therapist strives to maintain a position that indicates an interest in exploring all aspects of the problem, but prevents digression in order that the family can focus attention exclusively on how they see their situation and what changes they would like to make that would improve it.

The therapist's question can be posed in such a way as to be future- rather than past-oriented. The question: "What change would you like to make in your family?'' is goal-oriented; therefore it may move the family in the direction of taking steps to bring about change. Since effecting changes in the family system is the essential purpose of family therapy, the family and therapist have a common frame of reference to guide them during treatment. Less emphasis is placed on what brought about the problem and more attention is given to what the family can now do to work toward a solution of the problem. In general, a family therapist is not usually prone to establish a detailed history of the problem. Attention centers on what is happening here and now. Diagnosis and treatment are geared to the present and future rather than the past.

At the outset of therapy, the family will usually define their problem in general, nonspecific ways. Goals for change are also vaguely defined. Therefore, the therapist begins to ask the family to define problems and goals in more concrete and specific ways. For example, most families will say that they want a happy, harmonious family, but have some difficulty in stating exactly what would bring about this state of happiness and harmony.

This is precisely one of the problems. If they could find an answer, they would not be in need of help. As the therapist begins to insist on a more precise definition of the problem, the family is called upon to examine what is happening in a new way. Vague global answers no longer seem appropriate. The family is now engaged in the process of analyzing the processes of interaction that are the root causes of conflict and disharmony.

At various points, the therapist gives feedback to the family as it attempts to convey information about ideas and feelings. The therapist's comments are usually confined to asking for more clarification, at some points putting into words personal perceptions about the family's problems. The feedback may, therefore, contain some new information to which the family can react. In some cases, the family ignores or actively denies the therapist's comments, rejecting them as "off the mark." For example, when the therapist suggests to the Simmons family that perhaps the mother is asking for someone to help her, the father reiterates that she is simply upset with Eddie. This kind of exchange is useful insofar as the therapist becomes aware of what the family accepts or rejects regarding comments on certain aspects of family relationships and functioning. The therapist can direct the family to what seems important by asking for more information on a given matter or by turning attention away to another topic for exploration. In any case, the therapist must be more than a passive observer of family interaction, by directing and stimulating the process of information exchange to help the family define its problems clearly, in a way subject to evaluation and treatment.

The therapist works toward helping the family agree on what direction therapy is to take, and raises the question of what needs priority. Some families present three or four serious problems, any one of which could be the focus of treatment. To work on all of them simultaneously would strain the resources of the family and therapist. Therefore, the family is requested to decide which problem they want to solve first. Once this consensus has been achieved, therapist and family work out a contract spelling out what each party agrees to in regard to who will participate, the frequency of sessions, duration of treatment, and mutually agreeable goals. Family members are then asked to make a commitment to be responsible for carrying out their part, and the therapist agrees to help them work toward their goals' achievement.

In most cases, the therapist engages the family in bringing about changes in family relationships. A strong parental coalition is basic to optimal family functioning. Families in which each parent seeks power, so that the conflict between them splits the family into warring factions, are highly dysfunctional. Therefore, strengthening the coalition between father and mother has high priority in therapy. In the Simmons family, the split between the parents is not open and above-board. There are indications that the father remains aloof and uninvolved in family matters. He expects the mother to solve all problems dealing with the children. He seems unconcerned as to *how* she solves these problems and does not offer to come to her aid, except, as Eddie points out, "He just yells at everybody." The father also hints at a problem in his relationship to his wife. He sees Eddie as being in the way of establishing intimacy with her. The disputes over Eddie threaten to weaken the relation between the parents, and both of them perceive these disputes as having an adverse effect on the family.

Eddie sees his relationship to the parents and his half sister to be a constant source of frustration and anger. He regards the stepfather as less than a friend. He perceives his mother as being allied with his stepfather and against him. He points out that his six year old half sister is the family pet, and Eddie thinks of her as allied with the parents and against him. His position in the family is that of an outsider. As his stepfather suggests, Eddie does not feel welcome. Eddie's solution is to live with his real father where he would perhaps be accepted and welcomed.

The mother's position in this family network is more difficult than the others'. Her relationship to her husband Ken is being endangered by her son Eddie. If she moves in the direction of a stronger tie to Ken, her son will see this as an intention to oust him from the family, and will be even more alienated. If she forms an alliance with Eddie, Ken will see this as a test of her loyalty to him, and the conflict between the parents will be intensified. Attempting to straddle the fence, the mother has found this position of neutrality untenable in the long run.

The goal in therapy is to alter this pattern. Among the specific objectives are the following: (1) Help Ken and Eddie move in the direction of a mutually acceptable relationship. (2) Help the mother resolve her position by moving towards more intimacy with Ken, in order to strengthen the parental coalition. (3) Help Eddie move toward a relationship with Ken and his mother that ensures a reasonable degree of autonomy. A realignment of the family relationships along the indicated lines will result in the following consequences: (1) Eddie's acting out in the form of running away and his attacks on his half sister should diminish. (2) Ken's position in exercising power in the family will be strengthened and family problems will become a joint responsibility of the mother and stepfather. (3) As the alliance between Ken and Eddie develops, Eddie will become less alienated and will accept the parents' direction with less hostility. (4) The mother's position in the family will be improved with the development of an alliance between herself and Ken. Sharing the responsibility of parenting with Ken will relieve some of the strain she is under as "solo parent." (5) The half sister, Chris, may have some difficulty adjusting to the shift in family relationships, as her position as family pet is endangered.

As in any other case, these predicitons may not be borne out in therapy. However, the treatment plan is based upon observations in the here and now. As the therapist begins to work towards change in relationships, considerable resistance to change and periods during which progress toward these changes is slow and difficult to accomplish will appear.

Conflict in the Simmons family took the form of acting-out, namely, Eddie's being found at the bus station after a violent argument with Ken. The family does not deny its existence. The acting-out is a rather dramatic way to bring the family's problems to attention. The conflict does not take the form of psychosis or somatic complaint, but rather emerges in the form of a behavior disorder. The treatment of this symptom in one of the family members is directed toward helping the family cope with the conflict and resolve the problems that led to the disorder.

The family has not been successful in negotiation. In fact, negotiation seems not to have been tried. Ken has given Eddie gifts to solve the problem. He has also tried to interest him in baseball. These placating efforts have not gotten at the source of conflict. The object in therapy is to help the family use negotiation. In this case, the mother and Ken will be helped to resolve conflict in the following way: (1) Ken and Eddie will begin to negotiate with one another without the mother becoming involved. (2) The mother and Ken will negotiate in regard to matters that relate to their own problems as husband and wife. The expected outcome is as follows: (1) If the negotiations between Ken and Eddie are found to be useful, the relationship will also improve and hostility will diminish. (2) Eddie will have been included in the family and given a position of some respect in relationship to other family members. (3) The parental relationship will be strenghtened if the negotiation between Ken and the mother are useful and lead to a more intimate exchange of feelings as well as ideas.

These predictions are based on the assumption that family members will be able to negotiate the matters that now divide them. The therapist's role is to help the family learn successful negotiation. The outcome depends not only on the therapist's skill in helping the family negotiate but on the effective use of communication in resolving conflict.

Communication can become an important way to resolve conflict. Parties to a dispute "sit down and talk things over" to arrive at a settlement. This negotiation among family members necessitates communication, and each family member is required to state feelings and opinions honestly and freely during the process. Highly disorganized families afford no possibility for negotiation because the communication process is totally lacking in clarity. In the Simmons family, where this was not the case, there was a better basis for negotiation.

Enhancing this family's communication has a good chance of succeeding despite some obstacles, such as the mother's tendency to ramble and digress. The father's inattentiveness to the mother's communication is explained in part by her tendency to be obscure in her meaning. Her confused communications may reflect uncertainty and insecurity about her relationship to her husband. She is therefore less than direct and honest in revealing feelings, pain, and discomfort. This difficulty may very well be the focus in therapy, since the mother's lack of clarity may be a serious obstruction to bringing about changes in the relationship and in resolving conflict. With this in mind, the therapist may give some time to the mother and Ken's attempts at communication and negotiation with or without the children. Some sensitive areas may have not yet surfaced and will need to be explored in future sessions. The initial session indicates that perhaps the mother is concerned about matters that she has not yet spoken about. Her tendency to ramble could be her way of "talking around" a subject she feels insecure and is anxious about.

The role of the therapist is to encourage the family members to exchange open and honest messages in a clear way. This objective can be accomplished in the family sessions if the therapist consistently calls attention to a lack of clarity, confusion, or vagueness. By helping the family members present the meaning they intend to convey, the therapist begins to change the communication process.

Improving Individual Adjustment

A dysfuctional, troubled, or disorganized family system tends to produce maladapative behavior or personality disorder in one of the family members. In some families, a particular child becomes the family scapegoat, the one family member most adversely affected by unresolved problems within the family. The particular manifestation of the scapegoating process takes several forms. A school-age child may begin to have difficulty in learning or making friends. A teenage child may gradually withdraw into himself and become isolated from his family and from persons outside the family. An adult family member may show a marked personality change such as depression accompanied by suicidal thoughts or impulses.

The severity of the disorder in a scapegoated family member is indicative of the disorder in the family. A serious mental disturbance and malfuctioning such as schizophrenia usually indicates that the family system is in an advanced state of chaos and disorganization. The presence of mild neurotic symptoms or minor behavior disorders in a family member indicates that the family is experiencing some minor problems that create anxiety for the family member who presents the symptoms. In either case, the disorder in the individual family member's functioning is a signal that the family is not fully capable of functioning at an optimal level and needs professional help.

In such cases of individual personality adjustment, the task of the social worker is to identify the source of the problem within the family system rather than in attempting to explore the intrapsychic processes of the "manifest" or identified patient. Once the social worker helps the family recognize that the troubled member reflects problems within the family itself, the personality disorder is perceived differently and family members can begin to examine how faulty interaction processes contribute to maintaining symptoms in one of its members.

The following case study of a nine year old boy, manifesting personality problems, indicates how the social worker can intervene in changing family relationships to bring about changes in adjustment.

Gary, a nine year old, brought to the attention of a family service agency in a mid-western city, presented problems for the school and his family. Being obese, he seldom played with others on the school playground, frequently complained about being "picked on" by his peers, and was beginning to show learning difficulties. In the initial family session, Gary sat very close to his mother, while his father sat on the far side of the room. Gary's two brothers and one sister took their places between father and mother.

This seating arrangement indicated possible splits and alignments within the family — Gary and mother forming an alliance against father and the other three children. The physical arrangement of the family did indeed symbolize the emotional psychological divisions which separated Gary from his father and kept him tied in a highly dependent relation to his mother. All family members commented on their concern and disgust with Gary's immature behavior. He spoke in a babyish tone, clung to his mother, and whined when he felt mistreated or rejected. The mother recognized that his immature behavior was becoming a source of family embarrassment. Gary was always clinging to her wherever they went. She assumed responsibility for Gary's inability to mature. At one point she remarked, "I guess I have wanted to keep him a baby."

As therapy progressed, the father began to blame her for Gary's problems. He felt that as a father he had not been permitted to interfere with the mother's efforts to keep Gary dependent on her. He expressed dissatisfaction with his wife because "she has always shielded him from me." The rift within the family was now recognized by others in the course of the first four family sessions. Gary had remained close to the mother far past the time that other family members believed necessary. His siblings began to chide and ridicule Gary. The mother began to defend him, saying that the other children should help Gary rather than poke fun at him.

Gary's position as a scapegoat began to become more clear as the family laid bare some of the feelings not openly expressed before. Gary's brother voiced some jealousy, saying that he had never had his mother's attention and that Gary had no excuse for being such a "cry-baby." The mother said there was a reason for Gary's problem. As a young child he had health problems, including asthma. She had always been inclined to protect him because, unlike the other children, he was not able to play normally. As the mother spoke in his defense, Gary moved closer to her. When asked to speak for himself, Gary said he had nothing to add to what his mother had already recounted. He complained that nobody liked him. The father commented, "People would like you if you straightened up and started acting like you should instead of acting like a baby."

By the fifth family session, a picture of the family system began to emerge. Father and mother were split off from one another. In the process, Gary had turned to the mother for security and she had turned to Gary to fulfill her own emotional need to be close to someone in the family. She had found solace in this relationship and was reluctant to break the tie even though the relationship was seriously impairing Gary's ability to mature and function as a nine year old boy. The father presented himself as helpless to effect any change in this relationship. He also appeared to be unable to draw close to his wife or to Gary. In the eyes of his son Gary, the father was a fearsome person who threatened to take him away from the close, safe and secure connection with the mother.

The tasks for the family began to emerge as the pattern of relationships between husband and wife, mother and son, father and son were brought to light. A shift in relationships which would free Gary and open up possibilities for his growth and maturation was in order. The family would need to find a new basis for maintaining a sense of balance and homeostasis. To accomplish this goal, the family system would need to undergo some rather far-reaching changes. The tie between Gary and mother would have to be broken. To do so would entail some sacrifice for the mother and for Gary. To Gary, it could appear to be an unnecessary act of cruelty to separate him from the mother upon whom he had become so dependent. There would have to be compensations for this loss — both for Gary and his mother. For Gary it could mean being united with his father and being accepted by his brother and sisters as a more likeable person. For the mother, a break in her close tie to Gary could open the possibility of a new and more satisfactory relationship with her husband. To continue the existing pattern of relationships would leave the family split and keep Gary trapped in a situation precluding normal development.

The direction that this change in family relationships should take also became clearer. Father and mother needed to form a closer alliance if family unity was to be restored on a new and different basis. Gary would need to see his father as an ally, rather than as a threatening hostile person. The father would need to see Gary as a son, rather than as a rival standing between him and his wife. The mother's attention and devotion to Gary should be extended to the other children and shared with them. The two growing daughters could profit especially by the development of a stronger tie to the mother.

The Norton family indicated how family relationships become established and how they are maintained in a complex network of interaction among family members. Balance may be achieved at the expense of one family member who begins to show symptoms or act out family problems, as did Gary. To help the family change the pattern of relationships becomes the task of the family therapist, though resistance will usually be evident in the early phases. The family tends to stay with familiar patterns and finds difficulty breaking through barriers that have become established forms of relating to one another. Family therapy helped the Norton family break through an established pattern. Follow-up a year later showed that their efforts were rewarded. Gary had been accepted by his family, his need for a tie of dependency on his mother was markedly diminished; the opportunity to grow and mature was now open to him.

Changing Environmental Conditions

In addition to internal family problems, clients report numerous environmental situations that cause serious difficulties. Of these, inadequate income is by far the most frequent problem cited in cases that come to family service agencies and is indicated as a problem in three out of five families who sought help (Beck, 1973, p. 43). Unemployment ranked next, with one in five families reporting this as their most serious problem. Inadequate housing, poor job opportunities, and lack of recreational and transportation facilities were reported in one client in six.

The impact of environmental conditions on the family system is profound. Families subject to the constant stress of poverty, low income and chronic unemployment are highly vulnerable to disorganization and to serious problems such as mental retardation, mental illness, malnutrition, and poor physical health. Families hemmed in by ghettos and barrios, living in unsafe neighborhoods, who send their children to run-down, poorly staffed schools have grave difficulty in coping with the concrete practical problems of everyday living. They are also the families that produce the most serious social problems: delinquency and crime, child neglect and child abuse, and periodic outbreaks of violence.

Many, if not all, of these environmental sources of stress can be eliminated only by a serious effort to establish adequate social services for these families accompanied by a broad program of social reform that will guarantee all families an adequate income, decent housing, and comprehensive health care. The responsibility of social work as a profession to achieve these goals is clear, as is the commitment of the profession to the development of intelligent family policy.

Our nation's professed belief that the family is the cornerstone of our society is not matched by public policy. We have not really addressed the question of how to guarantee all families the conditions necessary for family support. We have no comprehensive health insurance program, as do Canada and many European countries. The inadequate existing income supplements for poor families fail miserably at providing minimum standards of living. As has been observed, we have poor programs for poor people. Commenting on the need for a more adequate range of services for families, the Carnegie Council on Children points out that ''The single most important factor that stacks the decks against tens of millions of American children is poverty. Other things being equal, the best way to ensure that a child has a fair chance at the satisfactions and fulfillments of adult life is to ensure that the child is born into a family with decent income'' (Keniston, 1977, p. 83).

Employment strategies need to be developed that will guarantee that all able to work can be employed at a decent wage. And there will always be some who are not employable. Moreover, in many single parent families the mother is needed in the home to care for young children. Other countries have found ways of supporting such families. Our nation has sufficient resources to make it possible for the children in these families to live in conditions that contribute toward their physical and mental well-being. The income support systems now in place are aimed at meeting special needs and represent a patchwork of support systems each having its own criteria for eligibility. None of them provides coverage for one of the most vulnerable group, the working poor. As a result, over one quarter of a million American children are found in families without a chance of providing a decent home environment.

Families dependent upon public assistance payments under the Aid to Families of Dependent Children (AFDC) provisions of the Social Security Act are the ones most people associate with ''welfare.'' It is the program most tax-paying groups complain about as the cause of skyrocketing government costs and higher taxes, whereas in fact, AFDC grants make up only 3.3 percent of all social-welfare spending. Payments to these families range from a monthly average of $50 per family in Mississippi to $346 in New York. In any case, the amount that is paid to AFDC families is usually less than one half the amount needed to maintain a decent standard of living and is far below the median income for families. The income of most families in this group does even reach the official poverty level.

The AFDC program has other consequences injurious to the family. In most states, the family is not eligible for AFDC if the father lives in the home. And in some states, AFDC will pay more to a family abandoned by the father than to one whose father persists in trying to support the children. Fathers in desperate financial circumstances move out in order that the children will be eligible for public welfare. The AFDC program also discourages parents from working because they lose their benefits if they accept employment. A family trying to support children on $4,000 per year may be eligible for some additional income from an AFDC grant. However, it will lose these benefits if the income received from wages goes above the $4,000 mark. Not only is the incentive to work taken away, but the incentive to break up the family is inherent in the very way in which benefits are determined. As the Carnegie report points out, ''It is hardly accurate to call a program that works to break up families and discourage employment a 'welfare' program.'' The report suggests that the present income support systems are poorly designed and in need of drastic reform. As a basis for implementing any income support plan, the following guidelines are set forth in the report (Keniston, 1977, p. 104):

- The plan should provide strong incentives to work. If an individual goes to work, the benefits would be reduced gradually, so that taking a job would mean that one's income would increase significantly.
- There should be adequate safeguards against abuse, and adults capable of working who are not taking care of dependents should not be eligible.
- A family of four should be guaranteed an income floor equal to forty percent of the median of families of that size, with adjustments for families of other sizes. Together with a guaranteed job, virtually all families would be raised above half the median income.

● The parent who has primary reponsibility for the care of young children would have a choice of working or staying at home, without creating strong incentives or penalties on either side to influence the choice.

Can the nation afford the cost of implementing a truly effective program to eliminate poverty? The Carnegie report estimates that an adequate income support program that would lift all families out of poverty would cost an additional $40 to $50 million. This increased cost must be viewed in relation to how income is distributed in the United States. The top fifth of families recieves forty-one percent of all income. The bottom fifth receives only 5.4 percent. In other words, a family in the top fifth receives eight times the income received by one in the lowest fifth, even after welfare payments. This wide disparity of income imposes an injustice to the millions of children who grow up in poverty. Responsibility for their future cannot be measured in terms of money alone; the ability to provide a decent life for all American families is not an idle dream but a vital necessity. "As long as our economic system permits millions to live in poverty," writes Keniston, "and as long as our political system is not committed to the elimination of poverty, no programs of personal reform, moral uplift, therapy, philanthropy, or early education can hope to eliminate the next generation that poverty causes" (p. 118).

In addition to income supports, a national program geared to promoting family well-being must include a wide range of other services relating to health, nutrition, education, drug abuse, and other special problems. There are a number of such programs now in place. Some are funded and operated by states and local communities, others by the Federal government. Most of them have been developed piecemeal. As a nation we have an inadequate and uncoordinated patchwork of support services that fails in important ways. Services are unavailable to many who need them. Others are fragmented and difficult to administer. Most services are designed only to *treat* problems. Few are aimed at preventing them. Almost all programs lack sufficient funding to achieve their goals. Finally, the second class nature of services for the poor stigmatize those families receiving the service, adding insult to injury.

The Carnegie report proposes that services to families would be very different if we started from a different set of principles, as follows:

1. *Universal access:* Services for all who need them would be the first principle. Everyone should have equal access and receive

equal benefits without regard to race or income. A comprehensive health insurance program is an example of such a service that provides access to health care for everyone.

2. *Racial and economic integration of services:* Some integration will follow with universal access to services in most instances since the services will be available without regard to income. Community service centers would offer services that cut across lines of race and class.

3. *Convenience and coordination:* A referral and appointment center should be available in every town or neighborhood, with the function of telling families where they can obtain services for their problems, make appointments, and provide transportation or baby-sitters if needed.

4. *Maximum choice:* Service systems should try to give families a choice among types of services whenever possible. For example, if a parent becomes ill, the children may need to be cared for temporarily. The parents should have a choice between day care, foster care, or center care.

5. *Parent participation:* To make certain that the way in which services are delivered reflects ethnic and cultural traditions, families who use the service should have an important voice in making policy and should monitor the operation of the service.

6. *Using paraprofessionals and volunteers:* In order to keep down costs and open up career opportunities to the unemployed, or those who wish to enter human services, the use of volunteers and paraprofessionals should be encouraged. Along with parent participation in planning and operation, the volunteers and the paraprofessionals will also familiarize the community with the services offered and make them politically popular in the communities that use them.

7. *Prevention:* A well planned program will be directed toward preventing problems from becoming serious instead of offering help after the damage has been done. It makes better sense to provide day care and other services that relieve stress on overburdened parents than to provide services such as foster care for abused children.

In addition to these principles, the report recommends that consumer councils be established on the local level to see that the services offered meet certain standards. Consumer councils would, first of all, assess the need for a given service. Second, they would determine whether the services are being used and are reaching the people who need them. Third, the council would evaluate the programs to determine if they are effective in dealing with the problems they were to solve, thus keeping agencies accountable to those who use the service and those who provide the tax funds or private contributions to operate them.

Family Advocacy

Social workers often find that the problems families must cope with are created by adverse environmental conditions that have a severe impact on their well-being. In an attempt to reduce the pressure of such adverse environmental conditions, the Family Service Association of America developed a program of family advocacy as a professional service designed to improve living conditions and to ensure that the systems and institutions established to help troubled families carry out that responsibility.

Family advocacy is concerned with the provision of a humane social environment for all families and adequate solutions of problems common to all families. Family advocacy grew out of the realization that many of the needs and the problems of troubled families are beyond the scope of traditional casework approaches. Unless resources are made available in the community, the best efforts to help families beset by overwhelming problems in health, employment, education and housing will bring about little change in the family's life situation. Although social workers are sometimes successful in working against these overwhelming odds, the demand for changing the social environment is clearly a mandate for social work as a profession.

The position taken by the Family Service Association is set forth in a memorandum to executives of member agencies;

> Most of you quite correctly may say that you have always been advocates for the individual and his family. Advocacy is systematizing for every family in your community the availability of prevention or cure of the problem you saw in that one family. Advocacy is, after finding the way to help one family, establishing a system that will get the same kind of help to every family who needs it (Manser, 1973, p. 61).

Most of social workers' advocacy measures grow out of individual casework situations that reveal the need for change in the community. An examination of the caseloads of family social workers bring attention to repeated instances in which the families served face common problems that cannot be resolved without active advocacy for the family to effect some important change to overcome the obstacles to solving the common problems. Whether the client seeks help with a problem in rights' violation or whether s/he seeks help with a problem such as unemployment, housing or inadequate health care, the caseworker should regard the problem as one involving the community's social institutions.

Where possible legal rights are involved, the social worker needs knowledge of the law and a sound working relationship with a legal-service agency or lawyer qualified to handle advocacy cases. The social worker also needs to be knowledgeable in other areas as well if advocacy is to be effective in helping the family. Becoming familiar with the credit practices of the community, the policies of school boards and administrators, the mode of operation of the psychiatric facilities and financial assistance programs are all important in developing advocacy knowledge and skills. To pursue family advocacy it is necessary to know the chain of command and how to file grievances with organizations involved in the issue. The advocacy process may involve working with several other agencies and institutions, as in the following case example.

A three year old boy was admitted to a hospital for acute lead poisoning; it was his second such admission in two years. The city health department had been called after the child was first treated. The health department investigation showed that the building where the family lived was so saturated with lead paint that it would be impossible to remove all traces of the poisoning lead without tearing down the building. The pediatrician who treated the boy refused to release the child from the hospital a second time without assurance that a safe, lead-free apartment could be found for the family. "If we get that child a third time, he will either be seriously brain damaged or dead," he told the social worker at the Family Counseling Center of New Haven, Connecticut.

The family service agency, the hospital where the child had been confined, and several other agencies began discussions with the health department and the housing authority about the problem of lead poisoning. An organization, Citizens Against Lead, was formed to work with the housing authority and develop a program to eliminate lead-based paint from existing housing. A bill was introduced in the state legislature prohibiting the use of lead-based paint from new construction and renovation of existing structures. The family service agency supported the bill; board members wrote letters and staff members gave testimony at legislative hearings, citing cases where lead poisoning had endangered the lives of children in the families they served. The bill was passed in a subsequent session of the general assembly.

Success in family advocacy depends upon the combined effort of the agency board and staff. The board must know the issues at stake, why the agency should be involved, and what strategies are to be selected in achieving the goals envisioned. The board should also be kept informed throughout the process and become active in policy decisions.

The professional social work staff of the agency must also become involved in the advocacy program. Among the responsibilities of the social workers, the following are deemed essential:

1. *Know your case:* When interviewing a family, detailed information about the total situation is carefully gathered to document the nature of the problem and the factors contributing to it. It is also important to consider both sides of a given case, to listen to both points of view and to determine if there is a strategy that will bring the opposing views into a workable liaison.

2. *Learn how the system works:* Find out how the institutions creating problems for the family are structured, who holds positions of influence in these institutions, and how the policy and practices of the offending organizations can be changed. Seek consultation from other experts to keep you informed about areas in which they have special skill in areas of law, city or state government. Work toward using the highest level of power in policy formation in order to bring about change within the offending organization.

3. *Work toward cooperation:* In any given situation, there will be other agencies and persons interested in working on the problem. Determine who is best equipped to help you in achieving your objective. Decide whether the agency or idividuals involved will be more effective in playing the role of leader, background supporter, or coalition member. Mutual exchange of information and point of view will prevent confusion and will enhance the chances for success in reaching advocacy goals.

4. *Check out your case:* Before going into action, check out your case to be sure you have all the information and documentation that you need. Be sure of the role your agency will play in the advocacy process, and know your potential enemies and friends. If the staff and the board of the agency are firmly committed to the advocacy goals and agree on the strategy to be pursued in achieving them, the program rests on a sound foundation.

5. *Evaluate progress:* If the goals are achieved, the agency board should be informed. The persons and organizations that co-operated in the advocacy effort deserve generous credit for the contributions they have made to the venture's success. If the advocacy did not bring about a solution to the problem, the situation must be re-evaluated, with a view to finding answers to these questions: What information was lacking? What unseen barriers arose? What mistakes were made in strategy? An evaluation can result in the formulation of a more effective advocacy plan based upon a revised view of the problems involved in implementing the original plan.

The effectiveness of family advocacy in bringing about change is illustrated in the following case of intervention in a slum neighborhood with a high rate of delinquency, school dropouts and an increasing rate of illegitimate births among teenage girls. The area had the second highest delinquency rate in the city. Over sixty percent of the families lived in public housing and were headed by single parents. Isolated by lack of transportation and with poor shopping facilities for low-income families, the area had been identified as a potential slum by the Office of Urban Housing and Development.

The Child and Family Service of Austin, Texas, recognized that the pressure of this environment on the life of the families living in the area was creating problems about which the community was concerned. The agency secured the support of a local foundation, the Rotary Club, and a mental health foundation in setting up a neighborhood project with a view to bringing about solutions to the problems of the area. Headed by a project coordinator on the family agency staff, the advocacy program began to focus on the lack of recreational programs, a factor that contributed to the high delinquency rate. In cooperation with the parks and recreation department, an after-school recreation program was developed for about 2,500 neighborhood children. During the summer months alone, 7,105 children participated in this new activities-for-youth program.

The problems of school dropouts and lack of achievement among the school-age children was a second area of concern. Volunteer tutors were recruited to identity individual student's learning problems. A summer school program of educational enrichment was set up for disadvantaged children to help them improve their learning ability during the summer months. A summer employment program was set up by community businessmen to provide jobs for approximately 100 young people living in the area.

The family agency advocate assisted the residents of the housing authority form a tenants' council to work on the problems of the project; the council was instrumental in sponsoring a clean-up campaign, securing additional garbage units and playground equipment. Lighting was provided for public areas and a section set aside for recreational activities. Through the experience of meeting together to work on common problems, the residents of the community gained an understanding of how to bring about change and improve the environment in which they lived.

The experience of the Austin, Texas, family agency and other agencies engaged in similar projects provides evidence that family advocacy offers agencies and social workers a way to bridge the gap between the many cases of individual grievances against social institutions and the broad-scale actions needed to bring about institutional change. The social worker's knowledge of the problems of individual families and his concern for the families he serves becomes an integral and vital part of the advocacy process.

References

Beck, D. *Progress on family problems*. New York: Family Service Association of America, 1973.

Manser, E. (Ed.), *Family advocacy: A manual for action*. New York: Family Service Association of America, 1973.

Keniston, K. & Carnegie Council on Children. *All our children: The American family under pressure*. New York: Harcourt Brace Jovanovich, 1977.

Weiss, R. S. *Marital separation*. New York: Basic Books, 1975.

FIVE

Helping Disorganized Families

The Watson family was referred to a family service agency by the Juvenile Court after the oldest son, Jim, had been placed under supervision because of truancy. Jim was one of six children in a poor family living in the inner city of a large metropolitan center. His father, an unskilled laborer, was often intoxicated on weekends. Recently his excessive drinking had become a serious family problem. His meager earnings barely provided necessities for the children, and his drinking habit was eating away at the money he brought home Friday night. There were frequent quarrels between Jim's parents about his father's drinking and his treatment of Jim's older sister, Eileen, an attractive, bright girl of seventeen. Eileen became the particular target of the father's anger during his drinking bouts. On many occasions, he had locked Eileen in her room, boarded up the door and forced her to stay there for several days without food.

The social worker at the family service agency discovered other problems as the mother revealed more about the situation at home. There were times when the children had gone to school hungry because there was no money until the next paycheck came, and the landlord was threatening to evict them for failing to catch up on the three months rent they owed him. Mrs. Watson, a self-effacing woman, had reached a state of hopelessness. Although she recognized that the family situation was worsening daily, she adopted an attitude of resignation. "Sometimes I think I ought to just take the children and leave,'' she told the social worker ''But then, where would I go and what would we live on? Our life isn't much, but it is the best I can do.''

Mrs. Watson's poor health contributed to her feeling of helplessness. Her legs were so badly swollen that she had to remain in bed for two or three days because of the pain. Eileen stayed home from school to take over the care of her younger brothers and sisters. An excellent student, Eileen had hoped someday to enter the state university, but that hope was now beginning to fade into an empty dream. ''I sure would like to go on to college,'' she told the social worker, ''but with things as they are at home, my mother needs me.'' Eileen had learned to accept her mother's resignation to the family's condition. ''She can't do much to change things,'' Eileen said. ''Not so long as daddy keeps on drinking. Sometimes I think I can't stand it. But if mother can stand it, I guess I can too.''

Eileen was concerned not only about her mother; she was also concerned about her brother Jim. She confided to the social worker that not only was he truant from school; she had found several articles that she was certain Jim had stolen. Among them was a transistor radio that Jim said he had found in an empty lot and a bicycle that he had ''just borrowed'' from a friend. Eileen's parents had not questioned Jim's stories. Eileen was afraid that soon the police would be investigating the thefts. Yet she did not want her mother to be worried, and she knew that her father would become angry if she talked with him about Jim's stealing. There seemed little that she could do to help. She hoped Jim would stop running around with other boys invovled in stealing and other delinquent acts. The probation officer had warned Jim that if he got in trouble or did not attend school, the matter would be brought before the attention of a judge and Jim would face the possibility of being sent to the state correctional school for delinquent boys. But Jim seemed rather unconcerned. He contined to bring home stolen goods, always denying any stealing.

Eileen's father had begun to drink excessively soon after his first marriage. The oldest child in a family of ten, Mr. Watson dropped out of school at the eighth grade, found a job as a laborer in a brick yard, and married at the age of seventeen. The first marriage lasted only six months. He married Eileen's mother four months later, and Eileen was born when her mother was sixteen. Mrs. Watson, also the oldest child in a large family, had been a competent student. Her marriage to Mr. Watson ended her schooling. A second pregnancy followed soon after Eileen was born. Mrs. Watson carried out her role as mother as best she could, even though she had become disappointed in her marriage.

Four other children were born into the family. By the time she reached her twenty-fifth birthday, Mrs. Watson was the mother of six children; at the age of thirty-six, she was tired, disillusioned and sick. Her husband had become an alcoholic at age thirty-seven. Her daughter, a promising student, was about to drop out of school. Her son was well on the way to a life of petty crime. All of her children sometimes went to bed hungry, and all of them felt alienated from a community that regarded such families as the Watsons with little regard, more often with contempt and disgust.

Disorganized Families: An Overview

The Watson family is one of many families that face severe economic hardship and are beset by serious problems of mental illness, delinquency, drug addiction, and other forms of social dysfunctioning. Social workers describe these families as "hard-core," "hard-to-reach," and "multiproblem" families. These disorganized families face overwhelming environmental pressures that weaken an already fragile family system. They are the families most vulnerable to stress and that need the most help in solving the problems of living.

Socio-economic background. The stress of poverty is felt by all multiproblem families. Poverty affects every aspect of their lives. They live in substandard housing. Their homes are poorly heated, vermin-ridden and in bad repair. Sporadic employment and chronic unemployment reduce their standard of living to the lowest level in our society. Family income is less than half the average national income. Fathers and mothers work at unskilled, low-paying jobs because they lack the education and skills necessary to compete in the job market. Many of these families depend on public assistance for extended periods, and most of them have been forced to apply repeatedly for financial assistance in time of crisis. For these families, economic security, the certainty that the future would provide for their children's basic needs, is never a reality, only a dream. In extreme cases, parents see their children go for days without food. Adequate clothing is a luxury they cannot afford. Whatever money they have must go to provide the basic necessity: food. If there is not enough food, parents go without. Malnutrition is not uncommon among both adults and children in multiproblem families. Inadequate diets lead to poor health, shortened lives, and early deaths for mothers and infants. Malnutrition takes its toll in mental retardation, as well as irreversible damage to the physical well-being of young children.

Children who grow up in disorganized families are often unable to make it through the educational system. Large numbers drop out of school without the preparation needed to earn a living. Some have above average intelligence; with opportunity and encouragement, they could complete their education and develop their potential. Lacking confidence, they become discouraged or disillusioned at an early age. Many of these children respond to help and encouragement. One expressed it well, "I'd like to learn and finish school. Only once you fail and fall behind, you seem to go on failing until you don't care anymore." Minuchin's study of disorganized slum families indicates that the children in these familes are handicapped because they lack the elementary skills in language and communication that develop in families where verbal skills are learned early and where communication is better structured. The life style of the multi-problem family also contributes to the child's difficulty in school achievement because the behavior of children from multiproblem families clashes with the accepted school standards. The family's value system is at variance with those of the community, and therefore children from multiproblem families are stigmatized. Their first contact with the school is often an unhappy, even traumatic experience for these children. Many of the problems of school performance are related to the problems of disorganized poor families. "We would suggest," writes Minuchin, "that the communicational, affective, and cognitive styles of the family members, as well as their aspirations, goals, and values are significant, not merely the quantity or quality of playthings or the variety of pots in the home. The habitual modes of child care, parental handling and the structure of the family system seem to be the crux of the issue" (Minuchin, 1967, p. 30).

Disorganized families suffer from social isolation. They do not seek out groups such as churches, clubs, or informal organiztions. They have few friends, and their contacts with members outside their immediate family are few and far between. Most disorganized families lack the simple skills that would enable them to join such groups even on the most casual basis. In describing the phenomena of social isolation, Young points out that these families actually fear all forms of social contact. "They fled from groups as they fled from all human relationships however diluted and diffused. In so doing they deprived themselves further of any steadying bonds, any contrasting pleasure in their nightmare existence" (Young, 1964, p. 37). Lack of social contact increases the children's difficulties in relating to others. Their introduction to the outside world is filled with experiences of rejection, alienation, and deep emotional pain. Having never been taught the skills that other children learn from their parents, they flounder and eventually give up attempting to make ties with others, thus repeating their parents' pattern.

Disorganized poor families are afflicted with major health problems. Chronic and acute illnesses are common. Many of the children are hospitalized for severe malnutrition and dehydration. Parents and children both suffer from a succession of infections that sometimes result in permanent damage and impairment. One major health problem is alcoholism. Young's sample of 300 families contained 186 parents who were severe and chronic drinkers. Other problems accompanied the excessive use of alcohol in these families. Arrests for drunkenness and disorderly conduct were common and 112 parents had a record of at least one crime, in most cases petty theft or other minor offense. The effects of family disorganization took various forms. Eight-two parents were sexually promiscuous. Forty-two percent of the children were truant. Of the 890 children included in the study, thirteen were diagnosed as psychotic and fifty-four as mentally retarded. Of the 300 families, 104 were one-parent families, thirty were unmarried mothers, seventy were divorced, separated or deserted. Thirty-eight percent of the parents had had at least one divorce, in contrast to the national average of about twenty-four percent. Some had remarried three or four times. As Young points out, there is much pathology in these disorganized families. "Yet the young still reach out for life and health," she writes. "They are hopeless only when no one reaches out to them. To ask them to be concerned for the standards of the community, to strive for independence when the community is not concerned for their independence probably is hopeless. The brightest spot in the bleak picture is the repeated indication that the children want something better, that they resign themselves to chaos only when the hope of order has been denied too long" (p. 40).

Family structure. The nature of the parent's exercise of power in disorganized families is confusing. At times, they use their power in an absolute, autocratic way to control their children's behavior. When such methods fail, the parents go to the opposite extreme by relinquishing power completely and handing over the responsibility for control to the children. Minuchin uses the terms *enmeshment* and *disengagement* to describe these two forms of family interaction. In the *enmeshment* phase, the parents are highly controlling. They are extremely fearful that the children will become unmanageable, and overreact to behavior they regard as unacceptable. Consequently, the children do not internalize norms of behavior, and the parent is able to control them only when physically present. The children in these families fail to develop autonomy. Parents interfere in every phase of the child's behavior. Children in these families become completely dependent on the parent's cues, and are unable to meet new situations without such cues.

In the *disengagement* phase, parents become unable to control the children's behavior, and turn over family leadership to older children in the family or to some external authority such as the courts. In some cases, one parent actually departs physically, while in others, one or both parents psychologically abandon the family. In these disorganized families the power structure is very similar to that of the dominated and chaotic families in the Timberlawn study. The enmeshed family power structure is maintained only as long as the parent or parents are able to maintain absolute domination. When that power structure becomes dysfunctional, the family system becomes chaotic. The leadership function carried out by the parents in healthy families is taken over by the sibling system in disorganized families.

Minuchin points out the tendency for family systems to get "frozen" in a particular pattern. He identified two distinct types of families: enmeshed families and disengaged families. In enmeshed families, the tight interlocking of the family members is resistant to change. All responses between family members are based upon the parents' need to maintain power at all costs, so there is little opportunity for the development of affection and shared concerns between family members. Almost all interchanges, are simply variations of power maneuvers. In disengaged families, the parents have resigned themselves to their inability to provide leadership. In a two-parent disengaged family the father is often ineffective. His inability to adequately provide for the family's needs places him in a position of inferiority and derision in the eyes of his wife and children. In one-parent families, the mother, usually overwhelmed by her responsibilities, has low self-esteem and feels inadequate as a mother and as a person. Often, not only physically alone, she is also abandoned emotionally and psychologically. The drain on her personal resources impairs her ability to assume the responsibilities of parenting, giving direction to the children, providing guidance and nurturing.

In most cases, the parents have themselves received only limited nuturing as children and their childhood models of parenting provide little to fall back upon to help them carry out their roles as parents. What appears to be indifference or apathy is in fact an inability to fulfill parental roles. Young suggests these parents' behavior is a reaction to problems they cannot cope with. "When life demands action, they cannot act — they have learned little from their parents but modes of escape. The most typical response to reality problems is to deny them, to run away from them, and to submit passively to the consequences. There is in all this what amounts to an abnegation of living, an acceptance of defeat so complete that action becomes irrelevant" (p. 36).

Marital functioning. Disorganized family systems revolve around a marital relationship based on the wish to be the sole recipient of love. Both partners tend to be extremely demanding. Neither the husband nor the wife feels that his or her need for emotional gratification is fulfilled. Frustration of the need for exclusive affection breaks out in various forms. The wife usually demeans the husband and relegates him to a position of inferiority and unimportance. The husband, denied the respect and support to which he feels entitled, becomes demeaning and hostile toward the wife. One or both spouses often act out frustration and anger by a series of extramarital relations to further humiliate the spouse; feelings of jealousy and mistrust characterize the marital relationship. Both expect to receive affection, but neither is able to give affection. They are primarily oral characters functioning on a childlike level and have great difficulty fulfilling demands to give as well as receive. Each looks to the other to meet the need for nurturing and parenting.

Although the husband denies that he wants mothering and protection from his wife, his dependence on her renders him helpless and floundering. He then turns on his wife, accusing her of robbing him of his manhood and placing him in a position of submission and inferiority. The wife in turn feels that she must stay in the marriage because her husband is helpless and cannot survive without her continuing help. The wife's sexual feeling for the husband is minimal or lacking in most cases. Her lack of interest in sex reflects some of her hostility toward her husband and reduces him to a nonentity, useful only insofar as he is essential to the wife becoming pregnant. The depreciation and personal devaluation of the partner is one way each spouse attempts to establish his or her own identity. The attacks are designed to bolster his or her own shaky sense of self-esteem by belittling and striking out at the other.

The partners' immaturity also limits their ability to work together on the solution of problems. Projection of blame is a common approach. The difficulty is assigned to someone outside the self. In some cases, each partner has an ill-founded faith that the other partner will somehow meet the situation and that everything will turn out well. Solutions are not thought out, tasks are not carried out, and the family continues to drift from one crisis to another, from one unresolved problem to another.

Parental functioning. In disorganized families the tie between parent and child is highly colored by the parent's own insatiable needs for affection. In some cases the relationship is one of outright rejection and hostility. In other families, the parent becomes over-devoted and makes the child completely dependent by discouraging emotional attachment to others. Mothers incapable of supplying a constant flow of affection toward the child may leave its care to others, or become so preoccupied with their own emotional problems that they have little energy left to give to the child. Mothers sometimes encourage children to become dependent on them as the sole source of affection and also encourage disrespect for the father. Fathers in disorganized families tend to give affection to their children inconsistently, vacillating between extremes of controling overdevotion and complete disinterest. Young suggests that perhaps parental indifference to this kind of behavior is to be expected because of the parents own childhood experience.

> Many of them had quite probably shown the same kind of childhood behavior for much the same reasons. The abnormality of the behavior would not seem so striking to those who had known little else and had small basis for comparison. When they had been children, their behavior had been their own problem and now the same was true for their children. Certainly part of their indifference stemmed from this. Even misery and deprivation can seem normal if one has known little else (p. 31).

Parents in disorganized families tend to overlook other families rules of behavior. The parents' behavior also suggests that the children need not conform to the expectations of society. Parents close their eyes to the fact that the children's behavior does not conform to social norms. "I know Mary is acting bad in school, but I can't do anything about it," or "I tell Henry not to take things that don't belong to him, but then he keeps on doing it anyway." Such statements reflect the parent's inability to transmit consistent rules of behavior and to all intents and purposes give children the right to behave as they wish without regard to expected standards of behavior.

Children in disorganized families manifest serious problems in adolescence. Adolescent girls tend to be submissive and to maintain a parasitic attachment to their mothers. They ignore their father's presence or show open contempt for him. Adolescent boys identify with their mothers and tend to use her to secure material possessions. The emotional attachment to the mother is resented by the father. In some families, the adolescent uses protective withdrawal as a way of avoiding close personal relationships with parents or peers. When there is a marked preoccupation with the self or with fantasy these adolescents are potentially, if not actually, psychotic. Moreover, the adolescents in disorganized families lack a firm sense of identity and capacity for self-direction. Voiland describes the problems of self-identity found among adolescents in disorganized families:

> For them, physical maturity proceeds but emotional growth is retarded, the ego retaining weak characteristics normal in a developing child but abnormal at this age. Society inevitably makes greater demands for more mature behavior than these children can approximate. As a result, self-esteem and identity are correspondingly and increasingly threatened and particularly at adolescence when earlier infantile wishes are renewed and the ego is in the process of becoming consolidated (Voiland, 1962, p. 257).

Pathology and family dysfunctioning. Psychopathology in children is a product of dysfunctioning family systems. A comparison with healthy family systems shows that disorganized families lack the positive characteristics found in optimal families and produce the most severe forms of behavior and mental disorders. The following factors explain the disorders.

1. The family power structure is extremely weak. Parents are incapable of forming a strong coalition and therefore cannot provide the leadership needed to maintain a smooth functioning effective family system. In the absence of a strong parental coalition, the sibling system takes over control of the family and assumes a position of leadership.

2. The absence of a strong coalition leads to confusion and family disorder. The chaotic condition makes it impossible for the family to function adequately in dealing with crisis situations and solving problems in day-by-day living. Therefore the family system does not have the stability to protect its members and to provide emotional security for the young.

3. The confusion and chaos in disorganized family systems prevent family members from achieving autonomy and a sense of self-identity. Boundaries between family members are established by processes of denigration and aggression destructive to the parents and the children, resulting in an extremely weak self-image that inhibits the normal, healthy growth of family members.

4. The affect in disorganized family systems is predominantly negative, with pervasive feelings of hostility between parents setting the family mood. This emotional climate within the family spills over into the outside world, causing the children to view others with suspicion and to reject accepted social standards.

The weaknesses in the disorganized family systems tend to produce serious problems for family members and for society in general. Among these problems are the following:

1. An excessively high proportion of children in these families become delinquent and are brought to the attention of authorities such as juvenile courts, police, and correctional institutions. These families also produce a disproportionate number of adults involved in minor criminal offenses and committed to correctional facilities.

2. The incidence of serious emotional and mental disorders in these families is found to be higher than in the general population. Many mental disorders go undiagnosed and untreated but are sufficiently incapacitating to impair the normal functioning. Alcohol and drug abuse is also a problem among such families, contributing to serious disturbances in the family system.

3. The marital and parental malfunctioning of these family systems results in the neglect of children due to the parents' inability to meet the emotional and physical needs of family members. The parents seem unaware of the serious nature of their children's problems and are inclined to ignore aggressive or withdrawn behavior. They seldom seek out help for those showing symptoms of mental or emotional disorders.

Disorganized families take an enormous toll in human suffering. The cost to society in terms of mental illness, addiction, delinquency and crime is also extremely high. Considering the severity of disorders in dysfunctional family systems and the cost to the family and to society, the need for an effective method of intervention becomes painfully obvious. Leontine Young describes the plight of these families in this eloquent passage:

These families walk our streets; their children go to our schools; their problems throng through our hospitals, courts, and social agencies. They are a part of our society, but too often they are as isolated from its main stream as if they lived on a desert island. Those who live in the slums of our large cities are hedged between the glittering prosperity of the commercial center and the tree-shaded comfort of the suburbs. They have no normal contact with either. They may look but not touch. Even when they are not slum-dwellers they remain apart, isolated by their problems and failures (p. 133).

The Helping Process

To undertake to help disorganized families is a challenging and difficult task demanding much skill and understanding.

From the outset it is important to recognize that disorganized, multiproblem families do not seek professional help voluntarily. They find their way to a social agency or mental health clinic only after some incident has come to the attention of another agency, and that agency requires that the family meet certain "minimal standards" in parenting and child care. The majority of families are either indifferent or hostile to sources of help in the initial phase of treatment. This negative stance has caused them to be labeled "unmotivated" and "hard-to-reach" clients. A professional approach to these families recognizes that they are resistant to help, but that responsibility for intervention must be undertaken in the interest of the children involved. Kadushin has pointed out that social workers must reach out to these families as troubled people, with a sympathetic understanding of their inability to cope with their problems alone. The social worker must convey an attitude of understanding and acceptance, but the family must also be led to realize that there is an element of firmness and authority involved in the relationship to the social worker. The approach to these families is based upon these fundamental assumptions:

1. The parents' behavior is not deliberate or perverse, but is due to the serious familial, personal, social, and economic problems that overwhelm them.

2. Although the parents seem to be grossly indifferent to their children's behavior, their resistance to being helped grows out of hopelessness and inability to change their lives.

3. Efforts to change the functioning of disorganized families involves reaching out to them through the use of home visits and persistent efforts to involve them in the helping process.

4. Traditional methods of intensive psychotherapy are usually ineffective. Intervention that focuses on the delivery of concrete services is required to bring about change.

5. The family's resources are inadequate to provide basic physical and emotional needs without the assistance of community resources. Therefore a wide range of social services should be made available to them.

6. Progress in treatment is apt to be slow and the goals in intervention should be geared to the ability of the family to effect change and should take into account the impact of environmental pressures that impede progress in treatment.

The approach to disorganized families "is one that combines acceptance and firmness, an attempt to understand rather than judge, and respect for the parents as people while in no way condoning their behavior" (Kadushin, 1974, p. 240). However, understanding and kindness are not enough. Since these families are highly disorganized, at times confused and belligerent, working with them requires a certain degree of firmness and authority to bring about change. Authority is used as an enabling factor to engage the family in the helping process, even though the forced intervention of the social worker arouses hostility, guilt, and defensiveness in the parents. Disorganized families do react to the fact that their adequacy is being questioned. Parents realize that their authority over their children is being threatened. Because of the conditions under which the treatment of disorganized families begins, parents will initially ventilate hostility toward any outsider who attempts to help them. Gross forms of denial of problems are used as defenses. Projection of blame on persons and events outside the family are also used as methods of avoiding responsibility for what is happening in the family. This resistance to help is to be expected. Disorganized families do not initially welcome assistance, but as the family begins to realize that intrusion into their lives is a demonstration of genuine concern and a desire to be helpful to both parents and children, the resistance begins to diminish.

Problem-Solving Approach

One of the most successful approaches to helping the multiproblem family is a problem-solving model that enables the family to untangle the web of problems it confronts to establish specific goals to be achieved, and develop the skills needed to solve their problems. Because these families have limited personal and material resources to bring to the solution of the problems threatening their well-being, the social worker actively engages in ongoing family life. By giving direction to the helping process the social worker engages the family in carrying out tasks resulting in positive and constructive outcomes. The social worker enables the family to determine which problems are to be the focus of attention and seeks to understand the problem in specific terms as early as possible. As the process proceeds, general problems will probably emerge. The practitioner then helps the client to identify the areas of greatest concern, checking to see what the family regards to be most urgent.

Specification of the problem is essential if the family is to bring about change: it must be spelled out in detail. To say that the father and son have difficulty in their relationship is too vague and general. Their difficulties must be described in terms of the interaction between them. For example, they quarrel every time the son uses the family car. Likewise, a family's statement that they are in debt is too general. The size of the debts, the nature of the accounts owed and the family's income must be explored to provide a limited and specific statement of the difficulty. For example, the family must pay $120 back rent by the first of the month or they will be evicted.

If the family can bring about some change in a relatively simple and limited area of functioning, they will begin to realize the good effects of therapy. However, if the family attempts to work on all their problems simultaneously, they become overwhelmed and feel powerless to bring about changes. As Helen Perlman has observed; ''The more beset the ego the narrower its capacity for coping. Thus some carved-out piece of what is felt as an overwhelming larger problem is less threatening to the person who has it; it feels more manageable to him. Within that piece it is usually possible to find a miniature representation of the whole'' (Perlman, 1970, p. 149).

After the problems have been explored and defined in specific terms, the practitioner and the family should develop a contract to set forth explicit agreements as to what is to be done and how. The contract specifies one problem as the target, the one of most importance to the client. A less important problem may be dealt with first because it is more pressing or because the family can solve it quickly.

Formulating the goals of treatment is the next step in the contracting process. The family and the practitioner state what they desire to accomplish. Setting goals calls attention to what needs to be *changed*, as compared to definition which states what is *wrong*. In some cases, the original formulation of the problem may not reflect what the client wants to work on at a later point in treatment. Flexibility is therefore necessary. Reviewing goals and modifying them when the family desires to change direction or to reassign priorities is an integral part of the helping process.

After the problems have been clearly and specifically stated, the practitioner orients the family to the treatment process and how the practitioner and the family are to work on the target problems. The family is made aware of what is expected from them and what can be expected from the practitioner. The contract should state the duration of therapy, the number of sessions, the intervals between sessions, and who is to participate in individual and family interviews. The practitioner must discuss the details of the contract and make certain that its terms are acceptable. Then the family is asked to make a commitment to work on their problems, using the worker's help to guide them to a successful outcome.

The problem-solving model was used to help the Watson family. They presented a number of problems in addition to the truancy which caused the referral: the father's excessive drinking, his abuse of the daughter, the forthcoming eviction of the family because of non-payment of rent, the mother's ill health, the son's stealing and delinquent behavior, the marginal family income.

The father's drinking was explored with the mother and the two oldest children at the first session. Mrs. Watson believed that Mr. Watson did not intend to stop his drinking which was becoming serious enough for her to consider a separation; however, this problem could not be worked on immediately. It was formulated in the following way: Mrs. Watson, thinking of separating from her husband, is not yet ready to make a definite decision. The father chooses not to discuss this problem and does not appear ready to work on his alcohol addiction.

The most immediate problem was eviction for rent arrears in the amount of $120. The landlord has not given legal notice, but has threatened to do so if not paid within thirty days, with the rest kept current from then on. The family will have to meet these demands or find a different place to live within the next thirty days. The family has no reserve to draw on to pay rent; its $100 per week income puts definite limitations on what they can pay.

The father's mistreatment of Eileen is a problem as long as he is in the home, particularly on the weekends when he drinks. Eileen must be protected from the father unitl Mrs. Watson decides about a separation. The question is whether the family wants police protection or chooses an alternative such as having Eileen visit a friend on weekends.

Jim's truancy is a long-standing problem. The school has discussed bringing the matter to juvenile court, but the authorities might postpone that, having made the referral to the family service agency. The school social worker, aware of the serious family problems, would probably cooperate in an alternative to court.

Jim's delinquency is a problem that might become serious. So far the stealing has not been discovered by the police, the probation officer is not aware of it either. The family fears that Jim will be dealt with harshly if his thefts are discovered and he is arrested.

The mother's health problem is chronic, but not serious. She has a private doctor, but is reluctant to get medical care from him because the family cannot pay for his services. They now owe him about $165, and although he has not pressed for payment, Mrs. Watson says that she cannot very well "keep piling up more bills." She has not inquired about other medical treatment sources, and is not sure that she would want to go to a free clinic for treatment. Medication, diet, and periodic check-ups are indicated to keep the swelling in her legs under control. The mother's ill health caused Eileen to miss school four days one month, which worries Mrs. Watson.

The family agrees that protecting Eileen needs to be worked on as soon as possible, not only for her safety, but because of its effect on the entire family. Finding a place to live was placed second in the list of priorities since the family could not possibly meet the landlord's request for payment. Mrs. Watson's health, to be dealt with in the very near future, was placed third in the list of priorities. Jim's truancy was placed fourth, and his delinquent behavior fifth.

The second session, attended by Mrs. Watson and the two oldest children, discussed Eileen's safety. The family considered alternative courses of action. Mrs. Watson found calling the police and having Mr. Watson arrested unacceptable. Eillen volunteered to stay with a girlfriend who lived nearby. Mrs. Watson eventually agreed to try this as a temporary solution. The practitioner asked the family how they would work out this plan. Who would approach Eileen's friend about staying overnight or for weekends? How would the problem be presented? Eileen looked to her mother for guidance. They decided Eileen would ask her friend for permission without giving particular details. Mrs. Watson would follow up by talking to Eileen's girlfriend's mother. They would say nothing about this arrangement to Mr. Watson, who would only become angry and try to keep Eileen from leaving. They decided to use this only as an emergency arrangement if the need arose. Eileen thought there would be no problem about going to her friend's house, and Mrs. Watson was in agreement.

The matter of housing was complicated. The family would need money to pay the rent at their new place, once they found suitable quarters. The social worker raised the further question of the family's long-range goals. Mrs. Watson hoped they could solve the financial problems that had plagued them for the past five years. The family had been moving on the average of two times each year because they fell behind in rent. Mrs. Watson had borrowed small sums of money from her parents from time to time to pay electricity bills when given notice that service would be discontinued. She had also taken out a short-term loan with a very high rate of interest. The outlook for improvement seemed bleak. Some steps would need to be taken to resolve the problem of paying outstanding bills and determining how the family would survive without a constant succession of emergencies.

The children's welfare also needed to be considered. Eileen had done well in school. Her teacher told Eileen she was an outstanding student who would do well in college. Her high school graduation was in six months, and she had thought of applying to the state university where the tuition was low and scholarship money was available. Mrs. Watson hoped this plan would work out so that Eileen "will have a better life than I have had." Eileen's goal was to prepare for teaching or some related field.

Jim's disinterest in school, his truancy and his delinquent behavior also concerned Mrs. Watson. She said she just hoped Jim "wouldn't end up in the Boys' School." Jim had no long-range goals. He said he would like to get a job and earn some spending money. Mrs. Watson thought their neighborhood might influence Jim's getting into trouble and being involved with the boys who "hang around the corner." Eileen agreed, and thought that if the family lived in better surroundings, Jim would not get into serious trouble.

The social worker reviewed the family's tentative goals. They wanted to get out from under the constant stress of being evicted and having to operate hand-to-mouth. They wanted a neighborhood with fewer temptations for Jim to steal and be truant from school. Eileen would like to enter college in the Fall. These goals became the basis for a contract. Some would involve long-range planning. Others could be accomplished within a few weeks. The family agreed to meet with the social worker for fifteen weeks, with the possibility of extending consultation if the goals had not been achieved at the end of that time.

Task Planning

After identifying the target problems and determining the goals of treatment, the family is helped plan problem-solving tasks for each member to achieve his/her goals. A plan of action specifies certain agreed-upon tasks, to be carried out by the family and the social worker. These assignments are not merely suggestions and become an integral part of the contract between the family and the worker that the family is expected to carry out. They help the family members achieve skill and autonomy in problem-solving actions. William Reid and Laura Epstein, who have pioneered the development of the task-centered approach, identify the following steps in planning tasks and in helping the family carry them out: generating alternatives; planning details of implementation; developing task strategies; establishing incentives and rationale; simulation and role-playing; analysis of obstacles to problem resolution (Reid, 1978; Reid & Epstein, 1977).

Generating alternatives. The family and the social worker all suggest a number of ways to solve a certain problem. This "brainstorming" can often be effective in working out tasks because it stimulates the family to think about new ways of approaching a difficulty. After exploring the alternatives, the family chooses those that deserve serious consideration, in some cases arriving at new methods of attacking a problem while attempting to carry out given tasks. These new alternatives can help the family develop new tasks. Reid observes that such experiments are useful. "Practitioners should not only be alert to these possibilities and try to build on them when they occur but should encourage experimentation with problem-solving. The tasks generated are often quite successful since the client has an investment in them and has already done some pilot testing" (p. 142).

The worker sometimes suggests alternative ways of approaching a problem, especially when the family is not able to produce them on its own initiative. The workers' special knowledge may enable them to suggest particularly effective tasks. However, the worker should not impose ideas on the family, but put forth suggestions for consideration and incorporation in planning.

Planning the details. After the alternatives have been considered, the family and the worker decide how the task will be implemented. Usually a given task can be broken down into smaller units of operation to accomplish the larger task. For the Watson family the task of looking for a place to live was broken down into several parts. Mrs. Watson would look in classified ads each evening and morning, calling to inquire about details such as amount of space, cost, availability. She would then sort out promising places within the cost limitation. Places comparatively nearby would be considered first; Mrs. Watson would make three visits each day to determine whether the housing met the family's requirements.

Eileen chose inquiring about colleges as her task, as broken down into smaller units: writing to the state university regarding costs and scholarship aid, talking with her counselor, and asking assistance in making an application. She would then talk with her mother and the school counselor together to determine whether a plan could be worked out for her to attend college in the Fall.

In considering assignments, the worker attempts to make certain that the action is not too difficult. "We have found," writes Reid, "that it is better to err on the side of having the first task be too easy rather than too difficult, since it is important that the client experience initial success in his work on the problem...The impression that one has performed successfully can create a sense of mastery and self-confidence that can augment problem-solving efforts. The actual experience of success is perhaps the best way to acquire this impression" (p. 145).

Developing task strategies. To help the family carry out tasks, the worker may set out a program of increasingly difficult actions and praise the family for successful completion of each of these tasks. If the family is unable to accomplish the original task, the worker can revise the plan and use smaller gradations within the family's ability. Some tasks involve cognitive abilities and require the family to give special thought to making a decision. In the Watson case, the family needed to decide whether separation should be considered. Mrs. Watson put into writing the advantages and the disadvantages of permanent separation. Working on the task helped bring out the issues she needed to consider. Previously unable to concentrate on the problem productively, she was now able to discuss it at family sessions and come to the decision that she would try a temporary separation before making the final break.

Establishing incentives and rationale. Families need an incentive and are better able to carry out tasks that they believe will be worthwhile. In some cases, the family is not certain that the benefits are sufficient compared with the difficulty and effort involved. In such cases the worker can strengthen their motivation by helping them envision the pay-off. Reid points out several such steps to strengthen motivation.

He may ask the client what benefits he sees coming to him if he can achieve the task. The practitioner emphasizes the positive consequences the client might reveal and explores for others. Possible negative consequences are examined and their impact considered. The client is helped to see the risks within the perspective of the gains that result from his proposed actions. If the risks still loom larger than the gains, in the client's mind, the task may have to be modified or another found (p. 155).

Another incentive for performing a task is receiving approval. Family satisfaction from completing a task is also a motivating factor. Such rewards give the family strong incentives to move on to more difficult tasks because they anticipate the approval of the worker who recognizes the value of what they have accomplished.

Simulation and role-playing. The family often needs help in carrying out unfamiliar tasks. Simulation and role-playing enables the family to rehearse the behavior and to perform the task under controled, nonthreatening conditions. Tryouts have the advantage of learning by doing in a simulated situation similar to the real and permits the family to act out the task behavior. This technique is particularly useful in helping the family prepare for interacting with another person in carrying out a given task. For example, Mrs. Watson was helped prepare for an interview and application for financial assistance at the local welfare department, after she expressed fears that she would not know what to say and that her application would not be accepted. The worker suggested that she would act out the part of the public assistance worker and demonstrate what questions would be asked. After the worker modeled the task for Mrs. Watson, they rehearsed the task behavior until Mrs. Watson felt comfortable and self-assured.

Analysis of obstacles. Families may delay certain tasks because they imagine the possible obstacles to be so overwhelming that the task cannot be successfully completed. The worker can help the family get through these barriers by detailed discussions testing out whether the imagined obstacles are really insurmountable, and suggesting how they can be overcome. For example, Mrs. Watson was reluctant to separate from Mr. Watson. She believed Mr. Watson would become enraged and cause trouble for her if she left him. The worker pointed out that the legal aid lawyer representing her could ask the court to issue a protective order. The worker assured Mrs. Watson she would be available in case of emergency. By anticipating possible obstacles, the social worker can identify fears interfering with the achievement of a given task. By removing those obstacles as planned, Mrs. Watson was able to carry it out.

Task Review. An important component of the task-centered approach are task reviews indicating which were completed, which partially accomplished and which that remain to be completed. If some parts of a task were not completed, the reasons are discussed in a non-critical way. Some tasks may be abandoned because on review they seem inappropriate for the situation or because the obstacles to them cannot be overcome. If the family has successfully completed a given task, it can perform a similar or more difficult one. When the family has completed all the tasks involved in the solution of the problem, the family is ready for termination of service.

The termination phase is directed toward what has been accomplished during treatment. The family is also encouraged to continue work on problems not solved, by using methods learned during treatment. As Reid points out, the task-centered approach is an effective way of helping families extend problem-solving to other areas.

> Key steps are put in nontechnical language and in a form the client can use on his own: narrowing down the problem; listing the various things that can be done about it; deciding on a course of action and planning how it should be carried out, including breaking large tasks into smaller ones; providing oneself with incentives; rehearsing and practicing what is to be done; figuring out what to do about things that stand in the way; and getting others to help (p. 82).

Using community resources. Multiproblem families need a wide variety of social, financial and health services because they face many problems and have limited resources to cope with them. Therefore, the appropriate and effective use of community services is an extremely important part of the helping process. The role that the social worker plays can be summarized as follows:

1. The social worker acts as broker between the family and the helping resource, linking services to the family's needs. Knowledge of what services are available, informing the family of the nature of the services, and helping the family to determine whether to use the service are basic to carrying out the broker role.

2. The social worker acts as family advocate, giving special attention to the right to receive service and representing the family in cases that involve rejection of applications for assistance. Knowledge of the regulations that control the offering of assistance and service and the capability to speak in behalf of the family are essential to the performance of the advocate role.

3. The social worker acts as enabler to assist the family in making maximum use of the resources available by pointing out how applications are made and how eligibility is determined. Helping the family gather the necessary information required is a tangible way of enabling them to use a community resource.

The Watson Family Revisited

The combined use of a problem-solving approach and community resources is effective in producing significant, long-standing change in the life of a family and its members, as illustrated with the Watson family over approximately one year. At the end of this time the family had accomplished many of its goals.

Mrs. Watson decided to separate from her husband and received a divorce through the help of the Legal Aid Services lawyer. The family accepted the wisdom of the mother's decision. Mr. Watson's excessive use of alcohol had become more and more uncontroled and eventually he was involved in an assault during a drinking spree and arrested. Released on probation, he is still working and makes a regular contribution to the support of the three youngest children.

The separation has given the family relief from the periodic episodes of violence that characterized their lives for more than five years. In addition to the father's support payments, financial assistance through AFDC program gives the family a small but dependable source of support. Mrs. Watson is enrolled in the WIN program and hopes to obtain employment in a local manufacturing plant upon the completion of her training course.

Eileen is planning to work during the summer to earn enough money to pay for her books when she enters the state university, where she obtained a scholarship covering the cost of tuition. She has been assured that the university will employ her as a cafeteria worker and Eileen will use this income to pay for her room and board. Mrs. Watson is very pleased that Eileen will have an opportunity to get a college education. The school counselor and the family social worker have planned a going-away party for Eileen and invited ten of her classmates. She will graduate at the top ten percent of her high school class.

Jim has made friends in the new neighborhood. He has not been in any trouble, and the probation officer has given serious thought to recommending that he be released from probation. Jim's mother had a conference with the school teachers when the social worker suggested that it might be a good idea to see what could be done to interest Jim in attending school regularly. The school reports that his attendance has improved. When Jim starts high school next fall, the social worker will help work out a program of part-time classes and employment because earning money is very important to him.

The future looks more promising to Mrs. Watson and her family. They live in a fairly comfortable house and although they do not have much to spend for food or clothing, they are out of debt and managing to meet their bills. It is a better life than they have had for a long time.

Shared Problem-Solving Tasks

Disorganized families have great difficulty agreeing on how ordinary everyday tasks will be carried out. Simple chores such as washing dishes, preparing meals, and laundering clothes go undone because there is no systematic way to carry them out. Recurring endless conflicts surround the issues of who is to do what and why a given task was neglected. Eventually, the family bogs down in a morass of bickering and total disorganization. The executive function of the family is weakened and the family flounders because no one determines what needs to be done, assigns responsibilities, and sees them carried out.

A joint problem-solving approach helps the family overcome these conflicts and enables its members to cooperate in carrying out tasks. With the worker's help, the family develops shared tasks to be carried out in day-by-day interaction. Agreements on these shared tasks can be arrived at during a family session under the direction of the social worker. The worker asks the family to discuss a specific problem, formulate alternative ways of solving the problem, and arrive at a contract specifying what is expected of each family member. This negotiation process is often time-consuming and tedious, as illustrated in the following example.

During a family session, the mother explained that the children had been absent from school for two days because they had no clean clothes to wear. The washing machine had broken, and they had no money to have it repaired. Meanwhile, the dirty clothes were accumulating, and the family had no plan for getting them washed.

The worker suggested that the family think of ways to solve the problem. The youngest child suggested they go to the store and buy new clothes, which met with derision from the older siblings. A digression followed. The oldest daughter complained that she needed new clothes. Another child said that he had been promised new shoes. The daughter countered that he did not, and that she was entitled to new clothes because she was a girl and boys did not need new clothes.

The mother remained uninvolved in the dispute, and the argument continued unabated. Eventually the mother became involved, saying that boys needed clothes just as much as girls. The daughter accused the mother of not keeping her promise to buy her a new sweater. The mother denied the promise. The son said the mother was right, but that she had promised to buy him a new pair of shoes. The mother said she had never promised to buy anything for any of the children and that they "could just forget about it."

This summary of its interaction shows a family may avoid coming to grips with a problem by engaging in digressions that take attention away from the task to be carried out. Responses are highly personal, characterized by attacks and counter-attacks. The original purpose of solving a specific problem is lost, with the family ending up in a state of confusion and frustration. During these faulty, nonproductive exchanges, children look to the parent to control the exchanges, bring the matter to a conclusion, and work out an appropriate solution. In disorganized families this leadership is lacking and the family drifts without coming to a decision about what they will do to resolve the situation.

Direct worker intervention is usually necessary to help the family cut through dysfunctional interaction and provide a framework for action. In the case cited above, the worker waited a few moments after the interaction ended without solving the problem of getting the laundry done. Then he directed the mother to take charge and try to work out a solution that would require everyone in the family to participate. He explained that sometimes things get done if everybody pitches in and helps. The mother said she had thought of taking the laundry to a laundromat but that it would not be safe to leave the younger children alone. The worker asked the mother to talk with the other children about how the clothes could be brought to the laundromat without her help. The family seemed at a loss. Eventually the son came up with an answer, suggesting that they put the clothes in a wagon that the children used to pull each other in play. The worker turned to the mother for her reaction. At this point all the family members began to talk about how this would work out. The conversation and exchanges were animated with many interruptions and not much attention given to what each had to say. The worker suggested that they listen to what others were saying. He put mother in charge of working out the details.

With occasional help from the worker, the mother eventually assigned responsibility to the children, making the oldest daughter responsible for sorting the clothes. The younger children were to help the daughter load the clothes on the wagon and go with her to the laundromat. Other details, such as getting the coins and supplies needed, were to be taken care of by the mother. The family was to report back to the worker at the following family session as to how well they had carried out their various assignments.

The shared-task approach has special value to the family because it moves them toward a joint effort that pays off. Certain secondary effects also prove beneficial. The family learns how to negotiate and execute a plan in which all members have participated. They feel a definite sense of accomplishment. Putting the mother in a position of authority and responsibility also restores the leadership necessary to solve problems and cope with reality. Although the worker temporarily took over leadership, he was careful to check every step with the mother and eventually put her back in charge of the family and the decision-making process.

This task-centered approach can also be effectively employed in planning enjoyable activities such as going to the movies or planning an outing. Enjoyable activity tasks are designed to give the family an experience that not only draws them together but also provides an opportunity to derive pleasure from their relationship. The worker suggests such tasks to break up patterns of withdrawal and isolation that the family cannot alter without outside help. The activity must be regarded as mutually enjoyable by all family members. If this is not possible, the family may reach a reciprocal agreement. For example, if an outing is planned to please some family members, a trip to the zoo can be planned for others. Such reciprocal exchanges make the family aware of the need to reach agreements about diverse activities and to satisfy all family members. In the process, the worker reinforces the family's ability to negotiate differences and to work out solutions through effective communication.

Problem-Solving and Communication

The ability of the family to solve problems depends very much on an ability to communicate, that many lower-class families do not have. Parents pay little attention to what the children say, and the children pay little heed to what parents tell them. Family members seem to accept the fact that they will not be heard. ''The result is a style of communication wherein people do not expect to be heard and in which they assert themselves by yelling,'' writes Minuchin. ''Conflicts do not have closure; therefore there is a faulty development of themes, restricted affective range, and a lack of training in the elaboration of questions to gather information'' (p. 201). Therefore it is necessary for the worker to help disorganized families learn how to communicate in new ways. Efforts are first directed to teaching them to listen to one another by requesting each family member to repeat what the other has just said to check whether messages are being received and understood. The worker may also actively control communication by stopping interruptions, pointing out that a particular response is not relevant. This enables the family to focus their dialogue on a single theme, so that the communication process is completed.

When the worker intervenes in the communication process, he challenges the family structure. He disobeys the traditional communication pathways that the family uses without posing explicit ways that the family could change their methods of communicating. For example, if the mother usually does most of the talking while the father sits by and listens, the worker may begin to give exclusive attention to the father, ignoring the mother. Or he may choose to reverse the usual paths by silencing the wife and urging the husband to interact directly with the children. These challenges introduce new processes of interaction, the habitual response patterns are given up, and the family can begin to resolve conflict in a different way. The family can no longer use the child as the scapegoat for all the family's problems; they must now focus attention on the faulty processes that are the actual cause of the conflict.

This approach to conflict stands in contrast to traditional forms of psychotherapy that focus on the intrapsychic aspects of conflict as a source of difficulty. Family therapy focuses on the interaction processes that are the source of conflict and helps the family deal with it by developing effective forms of communication. As Minuchin points out:

What the therapist does when he challenges the transactional pathways is to create new experience, the interpretation eventually becoming available through the process of blocking or curtailing the habitual pathways of interaction. The process is derived from the notion that the problem of the child is a result of certain organizational arrangements that the family and that the child, in collusion with the parents, maintains (p. 258).

Disorganized families are disabled but cannot tell the worker what is wrong. Confused and baffled by the conflicts tearing them apart, they do not know how to resolve them. They cannot clearly explain what causes the conflict or what to do about it. The therapist must make their difficulties clear and help them work toward solutions. Therefore the worker plays an active role in changing the family interaction. He moves immediately into the arena of the family's life as it struggles with conflict. The emphasis is providing relief for immediate distress and reducing tension in relationships. The worker's active role in intervention is particularly significant in helping disorganized families because their patterns of interaction are highly destructive and their methods of acting out to resolve conflict leads to serious problems for themselves and for the community.

Effectiveness of Problem-Solving

Traditional methods used in working with middle-class families are not effective in helping disorganized low-income families, primarily because they do not speak to the problems that incapacitate multiproblem families. Traditional casework concentrates on the subtle intrapsychic processes as the focal point of change. Disorganized families whose lives are characterized by overwhelming and pervasive poverty and who are coping with extreme external environmental stress need a different approach, directed toward the immediate resolution of problems and the alleviation of stress. Problem-solving and task-centered methods have been tested with a group of families in a research project conducted by William Reid and Laura Epstein. The project sample consisted of eighty-seven predominantly black, low-income families. The bulk of the employed adults worked at unskilled or semi-skilled jobs and had no more than a high school education. Most lived in deteriorated inner city housing, in areas plagued by high crime rates. Forty percent reported serious health problems; about the same percentage were headed by a single parent, usually a mother with young children. Twenty-four percent were receiving public assistance.

An experimental situation was used to test the results of a task-centered approach to working with these families. The control group was involved in traditional supportive treatment. The experimental group was offered problem-solving and task-centered casework service. The study found that the task-centered experimental group made significantly more progress than the control group. The criteria used to evaluate effectiveness were determined as making gains in solving the problems presented by the family during the course of treatment. Forty-two percent of the project cases in the experimental group showed progress as compared to twenty-six percent of the families in the control group. More than forty percent of the task-centered cases met the criteria of successful outcome of treatment as compared to about one fourth of the families that received traditional supportive treatment (pp. 241-42).

The effectiveness of task-centered casework was tested by asking clients to evaluate change after termination of service. This follow-up study showed that the overwhelming majority of clients (eighty percent) thought that their overall situation had changed for the better; the remainder said that their problem as a whole had not changed. Collateral sources were also asked to evalute the experimental families. The collaterals felt that the overall situation of sixty percent of the clients had shown a change for the better (Reid, 1978, p. 263).

Clients in the experimental group were also asked to rate their satisfaction with the service. Eighty percent thought that they could not have gotten along without it. An additional thirteen percent indicated that they had been helped slightly. Only one client indicated that the service had not helped at all (Reid, 1978, p. 265). The survey also indicated that one of the main purposes of the task-centered model had been accomplished, namely, providing the clients with a constructive problem-solving experience that would be useful to them in the future when new problems arose. Eighty percent reported satisfaction with their accomplishments and seventy-eight percent said they would seek the help of a social worker again when confronted with a difficulty beyond their own abilities.

The success of the problem-solving approach on working with disorganized families speaks to the essential purpose of social work practice, namely, to help people by enhancing their social functioning. This purpose is defined in a statement of the National Association of Social Workers: "To assist individuals and groups to identify and resolve or minimize problems arising out of the disequilibrium between themselves and their environment." A problem-solving approach that focuses on the immediate needs of disorganized families to cope with interpersonal and environmental crises shows promise of achieving that purpose.

Summary

Disorganized multiproblem families face severe economic hardship and confront serious problems of mental illness, delinquency, drug addiction and other forms of social dysfunctioning. They face overwhelming environmental pressure and are most vulnerable to stress. The structure of these families makes them exceptionally fragile. Parental guidance and leadership is often lacking, the family drifts from one crisis to another, unable to arrive at a satisfactory method of coping with the problems of day-by-day living, the care of children, or the development of a way of life that brings satisfaction and leads to productive enterprise. These families produce much personal and social pathology, an excessively high proportion of delinquent children, serious mental and emotional disorders in adults, and other forms of human suffering.

These families have been labeled poorly motivated and hard to reach. Progress is slow and tedious. Gains in treatment are sometimes discouraging, but with appropriate techniques, problems encountered during treatment can usually be overcome. One of the most successful approaches to helping the disorganized, multiproblem family is the problem-solving model that enables the family to untangle the web of difficulties they confront, to establish specific goals, and to develop a plan of action that will help them achieve these goals.

The problem-solving model proceeds through a series of steps: exploring problems, specifying the particular nature of the target problem, and setting goals. The family and the social worker agree on a contract that describes the tasks to be undertaken. The worker helps the family plan the tasks, and sustains their motivation to complete them. The worker also makes maximum use of community resources to help the family and acts as social broker, enabler and advocate.

The problem-solving model also enables the family to develop skills in communication and negotiation. The role of the worker is to change the family's habitual methods of communication and to help the family engage in shared-task assignments. Through repeated efforts at problem solving the family learns to apply what they learn in therapy to the solution of future problems.

References_____

Haley, J. *Problem-solving therapy*. San Francisco: Jossey Bass, 1976.

Kadushin, A. *Child welfare services*. New York: MacMillan, 1974.

Minuchin, S. *Families of the slums*. New York: Basic Books, 1967.

Perlman, H. *Social casework: A problem solving process*. Chicago: Chicago University Press, 1957.

Reid, W. *Task-centered systems*. New York: Columbia University Press, 1978.

Reid, W. & Epstein, L. *Task-centered casework*. New York: Columbia University Press, 1972.

Voiland, A. et al. *Family casework diagnosis*. New York: Columbia University Press, 1962.

Young, L. *Wednesday's children*. New York: McGraw-Hill, 1964.

SIX

Working with Abusive Families

The use of violence against children is not new. A parent's right to whip and punish children is implicit in the the biblical injunction, "Spare the rod and spoil the child." The Calvinist belief that infants are born totally depraved and sinful by nature is a development of this motto. Consequently, parents must vigilantly guard children against their depraved impulses and enforce absolute obedience to secure the child's salvation. To ensure submission to the parent's will, the child had to be "broken for his own good" even if this meant whipping, tying children to bedposts, or shutting them up in solitude and darkness. In some communites, "stubborn child laws" were passed, giving parents the right to kill children beyond their ability to control.

Although many children were abused since the first families came to the New World, Americans have not given serious attention to the widespread violence against children until the last twenty years. In 1962 C. Henry Kempe and his associates called attention to the severe injuries inflicted on children by their parents. Kempe's work sparked investigations among others interested in child welfare and led to the passage of child protection laws in all fifty states by the end of the 1960's. Under these laws, it became mandatory to report all cases of child abuse. Programs for the treatment of the abused child and his family were organized. The National Center for Child Abuse was established to inquire into the causes of child abuse and to develop programs to prevent the use of violence against children.

Stories about parents who inflict severe physical injury on their children find their way into newspaper headlines and television screens. In Paterson, New Jersey, a two year old boy was brought to the hospital emergency room. He had been beaten by his father and was bleeding profusely from injuries to his head and body. Doctors found that the boy's kidneys had been severely damaged by the blows; he died ten minutes after he arrived at the hospital. Physicians on emergency service wards report children so badly burned that their legs, arms and faces are swollen to twice normal size. Others bear scars and bruises inflicted by beatings with belts, lampcords or fists. Many of these abused children are infants under six months of age. A two month old infant was struck and banged against the wall because the parent found his crying irritating. A nine month old baby girl was slapped and knocked to the floor because she soiled her pants. The list continues indefinitely, describing injuries inflicted by parents, injuries that all too often result in death.

Such stories shock most people, but physical punishment is still widespread. Some form of physical punishment is used by eighty-four to ninety-seven percent of all parents at some time in the child's life, according to several recent studies. The most likely victims of abuse are the smallest and weakest family members. But physical punishment does not end when the child begins to walk or talk. Half the students questioned in colleges and universities said their parents had used or threatened physical punishment when they were seniors in high school.

A recent study by the Family Violence Research Program at the University of New Hampshire found that seventy-three percent of the respondents reported some form of violence on their children at some point and sixty-three percent of those with children between ages of three and seventeen mentioned a least one violent episode during the past year. Parental violence took various forms, the milder ones being most frequent; nevertheless researchers concluded that "the figures for extreme forms of violence yield an astoundingly high number of American children who were kicked, punched, beaten up, threatened with a knife or gun, or had a gun or knife used on them" (Strauss, 1980, p. 61). The study led to the conclusion that between 1.4 and 1.9 million children are subject to physical injury from their parents in any one year.

On the basis of a nationally representative sample, the New Hampshire study demonstrated that violence toward children goes beyond the bounds of ordinary punishment. "Millions of children each year face parents who are using forms of violence that could grievously injure, maim, or kill them," writes Strauss. "In many families these episodes of violence are not merely one-shot outbursts. They are regular patterned behavior which parents use to deal with confict with their offspring. We do not mean to imply that the majority of parent/child exchanges are violent; rather we mean that many children periodically experience beatings, kicks and punches in their homes" (Strauss, 1980, p. 73).

The enormous amount of permanent injury inflicted on the victims of child abuse is cause for serious concern about those who grow up in violent families. In addition to the danger of physical damage to the child, there is the impact of violence on psychological and emotional development. A study of fifty abused children at the National Child Abuse Center in Denver revealed that sixty-six percent had a marked incapacity to enjoy life, sixty-three percent manifested some type of psychiatric symptom, and thirty-eight percent presented learning difficulties (Martin, 1976, pp. 108-110). Most such children had a long history of parental rejection and emotional deprivation. Many had been removed from natural families to a hospital and from the hospital to foster homes. Abrupt and frequent changes in the environment of abused children undoubtedly interferes with normal development and causes problems in later life.

Children's early life experiences and relationships to their parents affect the way in which they mature and develop. Abused children develop a very poor self-image because of the mistreatment and rejection associated with their childhood. Abused children feel that their parents do not like them. Nor can they develop feelings of trust toward their abusing parents. Out of this background, children usually develop a strong sense of inferiority and low self-esteem. Some react by becoming withdrawn, passive and overly compliant. Others revert to infantile behavior such as thumb-sucking, wetting their pants and excessive crying. In some cases, the abused child becomes overly aggressive, provokes fights and bullies other children.

Violence Begets Violence

Genuine concern about child abuse goes beyond the immediate consequences to the child to the victim's subsequent behavior in adult years. Violent behavior is a learned form of conduct, transmitted from one generation to the next. Research on violent and irrational murderers reveal they experienced more frequent and severe violence as children than brothers who did not commit homicide. Examinations of presidential assassins or would-be assassins also uncover histories of a violent upbringing. In his diary Arthur Bremer, who attempted to assassinate former Alabama governor George Wallace, wrote, "My mother must have thought I was a canoe, she paddled me so much" (Strauss, 1980, p. 74). Lee Harvey Oswald, Sirhan Sirhan and Charles Manson all experienced violent childhoods.

A study of San Quentin inmates found that they all experienced some form of extreme violence as children. Psychologist Ralph Welsh claims that he has never examined a violent juvenile delinquent who did not come from an extremely violent background. As Murray Strauss points out, "Evidence seems to support the notion that our homes and how we raise our children are the main sources of our violent society" (p. 74). "Millions of our children," Strauss continues, "are time bombs of violence which can explode at home, at school, or in the streets."

There is strong evidence to support the conclusion that punishing parents produce violent children. Parents who are subjected to a great deal of physical punishment as children have the highest rates of abusive violence toward their own children. A survey by Strauss and his associates indicates a clear relationship between childhood punishment and abusing parenthood. Mothers punished physically as teenagers were likely to inflict serious injury on their own child. One out of four such mothers inflicted child abuse. As with mothers, twenty-five percent of the fathers hit most often by their parents use violence against their children. Some abusing parents have been the witnesses to extreme violence between their own parents. The rate of abusive fathers who grew up in violent homes is about double that of those who grew up in nonviolent homes. Mothers abused as children who also witnessed violence between their parents showed a rate of child abuse of thirty percent (Strauss, 1980, p. 114). In contrast, less than one of four hundred of the children whose parents did *not* hit them used violence against their own children.

The statistics strongly suggest that each generation learns to be violent by an exposure to violence in his own family. Within an environment where violence is a part of everyday living, it tends to become accepted as a way of relating to other family members and even to people outside the family, as illustrated in the statement of a thirty-three year old convict imprisoned for violent assaults:

Violence is in a way like bad language — something that a person like me's been brought up with, something I got used to very early on as a part of the daily scene of childhood, you might say. I don't recoil from the idea, I don't have a sort of inborn dislike of the thing like you do. As long as I can remember, I've seen violence in use all around me. My mother hitting the children; my brothers and sister all whacking our mother or other children; the man downstairs bashing his wife (Strauss, 1980, p. 121).

The lesson that the abusing parent teaches his child by example is indeed a powerful one. Children model their behavior after that of their parents. When a parent hits a child, the child is taught that the use of force between family members is not only justified but morally right.

Social Stress and Child Abuse

Researchers have studied abusing families to determine whether certain characteristics are peculiar to families in which child abuse occurs and to discover what kind of problems produce violence against children.

Social stress is one significant factor associated with families that abuse children. Number of children is one criterion for measuring stress as the care involved in rearing children makes demands on parents' time and energy. The New Hampshire study found a fifty percent higher rate of violence among parents with two children than with one; the highest rate of child abuse comes with five children. Thereafter, the rate goes down though still quite high for homes with seven children. The explanation for increased rates of abuse in larger families seems related to the increased strain on the family to provide for each additional child, though surprisingly, families with eight or nine children seldom abuse them.

Gil's study of the economic and educational background of abusing parents showed that most of them came from low-income, poorly educated families; fifty-five percent had not finished high school, forty-eight percent of the fathers were unemployed. Serious abuse was found to be overconcentrated among the poor. Life in poverty and ghettos creates special stresses, more likely to result in child abuse. The New Hampshire study gives a somewhat different picture, showing that the families in the $6,000 to $20,000 per year income bracket are actually more prone to react violently to stress than the very poorest or most affluent families. The report speculates that middle-income families struggle with every stressful event because they are not well enough off to have financial security, and they tend to resort to violence under increased stress. The report points out that the rates for violence among the poor is already high and they would have to undergo a major crisis in order for the rates to go still higher (Strauss, 1980, p. 189).

Most investigations show that income has a direct bearing on the level of violence. However, most research is based on officially reported cases; there is reason to believe that poor families are more likely to be caught in deviant acts than upper-income families.

Unemployment or part-time employment is closely associated with child abuse. The New Hampshire report indicates that children whose fathers are employed part-time are nearly twice as likely to be victims of severe violence than children whose fathers hold full-time jobs. Not being able to hold down a full-time job often creates problems for the father because his status is in part dependent on providing adequately for his family. The father's unemployment also results in loss of income and financial difficulties that strain family relationships.

Stress is also related to various kinds of crisis situations. The more severe and frequent the crisis, the greater the stress on the family. Some life events, such as having a child, produce demands on parents and the parents will not always be able to respond adequately to these demands. The result is an increased level of stress. Given this basic principle, it would seem probable that families experiencing severe stress most often are also most likely to use violence against their own children. The New Hampshire study indicates a close relationship between stress and abuse. Using a scale of eighteen stress-producing items, the families involved in abuse reported a much higher number of stressful events in the previous year, especially among those reporting ten or more problems. The most frequently reported major problems were death of someone close, serious health or behavioral problems, or problems relating to the work situation.

An investigation by Blair and Rita Justice also found abusing families more subject to severe and frequent life crises than non-abusing families. Using a social readjustment scale to measure the impact of such life events as death, divorce, separation and sexual difficulties, the Justice study showed that twenty-two out of the thirty-five families had undergone a moderate or major life crisis compared to five out of twenty-five nonabusing families (Justice, 1976, p. 46). Abusing parents were faced with not only one crisis situation but by a repeated series of critical events. A rapid succession of crisis events appears to be significant because the family does not have sufficient time to recover from one crisis before having to cope with a new critical event. The emotional resources of family members are thereby exhausted, and when the stress becomes overwhelming, children become the victims of violence.

A succession of crisis events has a ripple effect on the family, limiting the capacity of the family system to absorb their impact. For example, the unemployed father begins to feel the pressure of debts and is subjected to covert criticism from his wife and other people in his environment who may hold him in low regard. The financial stress and psychological problems growing out of the unemployment situation lead in turn to difficulties in the marital relationship. Strained marital relationships cause problems in sexual adjustment. Lack of affection and support between marital partners produces feelings of frustration and anger. The unresolved difficulties mount and the level of dissatisfaction becomes intolerable. The outbreak of violence against a marital partner or child, perceived as the cause of the problem, is a frequent outcome of the frustration.

Dysfunctions in Abusing Families

Abusing families have serious problems in major areas including marital functioning, parent/child relationships, communication and negotiation. They also manifest a lack of knowledge about child development and child-rearing practices.

In abusing families the marital relationship is often characterized by a high degree of symbiotic attachment. Highly dependent on the other for love and other forms of emotional gratification, neither partner can function autonomously. Yet neither is able to provide the requested emotional support because each has been emotionally deprived in childhood. For parents unable to cope with the demands of the marital relationship, the child becomes the person from whom emotional gratification is derived. Therefore, the child is perceived as the one who will fulfill the parent's own unfulfilled childhood needs.

In such cases neither parent is capable of meeting the demands made on him or her to deal with the problems of day-to-day living. Decisions are delayed, problems go unattended or are denied. Passivity becomes the way to deal with problem situations. Individual responsibility or joint decision-making is lacking; problems continue to mount. Inadequacies in parenting are often denied even though there is evidence of child abuse. The process of discounting the problem's existence or discounting its significance takes the place of rational thinking or eventual resolution.

In healthy families, parents have a strong sense of responsibility to care for and safeguard their children. In abusing families, this sense of responsibility is lacking. The father looks to the mother to make decisions. The mother feels inadequate to use her own judgment;

she reacts by doing nothing. The mother finally turns to the father and asks him to take charge and resolve the problem in any way he sees fit. The father is told to "make the child mind" or the mother is told to "keep the baby from crying."

When rational approaches to dealing with interpersonal relationships are not available, other forms of control are substituted. As Strauss points out, violence is often used as a way to control the behavior of family members. He states:

> One of the very first things we recognized when we began to study violence in the American family was that violence is often used as a mechanism to control the behavior of family members. Parents often use violence and force to influence and control the behavior of their children. Frequently, perhaps usually, this force is used with the best interest of the child in mind. But, in other instances, the conflict between parent and child is one of pure confrontation where only who wins matters (p. 190).

In studying the relationship between spouse abuse and child abuse in the same family, the study concluded significantly that violent husbands and wives are likely to be child-abusing parents. Couples who did not hit each other had the lowest rate of violence toward their children. On the other hand, couples violent toward each other also inflicted abuse on their children in twenty-eight percent of the cases (Strauss, 1980, p. 115). These findings substantiate the view that abusing families are families with serious marital problems, often resolved by acts of violence, not only against the partner but also against the child.

Observers have also noted the relationship between the parent and the abused child to be a significant factor in many cases of child abuse. For example, nurses and physicians find that mothers hold these children in awkward positions that prohibit direct contact between themselves and their infants. Rough handling and a stiff, inflexible posture also give a message of rejection to the young infant. Sensitive to the emotionally cold environment, the infant becomes withdrawn and avoids close contact with the parents.

In some cases, the parents see a reflection of themselves in the child who has become the target of their aggression. Faults that parents cannot tolerate in themselves are seen in the child and often exaggerated far out of proportion to their real importance. Burdened by feelings of inadequacy and plagued by doubts about their own worth, abusing parents punish the child for trivial matters, bits of behavior, mannerisms and physical traits that are not problems for emotionally mature parents who have accepted some degree of imperfection in themselves as well as in others.

Abusing parents also seem to have little sound knowledge about child development. Much of the injury inflicted on very young children is in part caused by the parent's failure to understand that certain forms of behavior are part of the child's normal growing up. Abusing parents frequently spank or use some other form of physical punishment if the baby cries when hungry or uncomfortable. Young children have been subjected to the extreme pain of being immersed in hot water or placed on a hot burner for soiling their pants though they have not yet reached an age when bowel control could possibly have been established. Most of these unrealistic expectations can be traced to a combination of confused or inaccurate knowledge about the various stages of growth and development in addition to an inability to tolerate the problems associated with these stages. In some instances, the parents express the view that the child is deliberately behaving in a certain objectionable way to irritate them, so the child deserves to be dealt with harshly in order to correct this bad behavior. Parents justify their anger and extreme corrective measures on the grounds that they are necessary to bring about compliance and obedience.

Extreme punishment can often be traced to the abusing parent's own experience as a child and an attempt to simply use one's own parents' corrective measures. Such parents, even if they have vowed to never treat their children in the same way, end up becoming just as violent as their parents with their own children. Sometimes these same parents are alarmed by their own capacity to inflict serious injury on their children as illustrated in the following statement of a mother to a New Hampshire newspaper.

> When I was a child, my stepfather beat me. He beat me often enough to prompt me to swear that when I had kids I wouldn't lay a hand on them.
>
> It didn't work that way. The first couple of years everything went fine, then Bob (her husband) began making frequent and lengthy trips out of town. After he was gone a few days, I started taking it out on the kids.
>
> When Bob would ask me why the kids were black and blue, I would pass it off by saying that they fell while playing. Or bumped into a door.

As time passed, I would work out elaborately detailed stories to answer his questions of the injuries or the bandages. I would never take the kids to the same hospital or doctor twice. I would never use the same name. I even paid the bills in cash so I wouldn't have to give anyone my address (*New Hampshire Times,* February 12, 1975, p. 4).

The problem of child abuse is complicated. Violence against children cannot be traced to any *one* source. In some cases, serious overwhelming crisis situations are the immediate cause of abuse; in others, circumstances surrounding the child's birth or personality give rise to parental violence. The parent's own experience as a child growing up in violent family certainly contributes to his or her pattern of interaction with the abused child.

Families having serious difficulties in the performance of social roles, as parents or as marital partners, are apt to produce child abuse. Family members' inability to remain autonomous also contributes to a tendency toward violent behavior. Failures in communication and problems in negotiation of differences through rational methods with regard for the opinions and rights of other family members is also a strong contributing factor. The need to resort to force to control behavior and an inability to use alternative approaches to child management underlie all cases of child abuse. To bring about changes in families that are abusing their children and to help them develop nonviolent methods of coping with problems is one of the important aspects of social work intervention.

Approach to Helping

The inital phase of working with the abused child and his family is crucial. Social workers often share the general reaction to abusing parents and find it difficult to be sympathetic toward the mother or father who has inflicted injury on the child. These attitudes and personal feelings can interfere with the development of a helpful relation to the abusing family and the abused child. A relationship of trust and cooperation can be established if the social worker attempts to see the problem from the parents' point of view. They are desperately trying to cope with problems beyond their present capacity. Accordingly, statements such as ''Your child must be very difficult for you to deal with,'' or 'I think that you are really tring to do the best you can for your children'' will give the parents assurance that you are there to help them rather than blame them. From the parent's point of view, the *child,* not the parent, is the problem. The social work guideline, "start with where the client is" applies in working with abusing parents.

The following "do's and don'ts" are suggested as guidelines in approaching the parents in a positive way:

- Let the parents know you are interested in their problems. Don't play the role of detective trying to catch them abusing the child.
- Ask the parents how they plan to work on the problem. Don't pretend to have all the answers.
- Look for the good things the parent does. Do not call attention to all the wrong things done in the past.
- Give credit for the things the parent has been able to achieve. Don't tell them about how much they still need to accomplish.
- Assure the parents that your goal is to hand over the care of their children to them and that you will help them achieve this goal one step at a time.

After the relationship between the social worker and the family has been established, the helping process can get underway. An important phase of the helping process involves an assessment of the family of the abused child. The assessment inquires into how parental roles are perceived by family members and how they carry out parental responsibilities, including discipline, routine physical care, and management and behavioral problems. Observations about the marital situation are extremely useful. If the parents are divided or if they are emotionally distant from each other, the assessment can indicate how the marital dissatisfaction is involved in the abuse of the child. A brief study of the history of the child and his place in the family can also provide important clues. The relationship between the child and the parents may be related to the reactions of the mother or father to the pregnancy or to the bonding experience between mother and child during early infancy.

The assessment process inquires into the most frequent sources of conflict between family members and how they attempt to resolve the conflict. Information about how family members try to communicate and how they attempt to convey thoughts and feelings to each other is an essential part of the study. Through observation the social worker can help the family identify obstacles to free and open communication in an effort to help the members adopt new and more effective ways of interacting. Alignments and splits among family members can also be carefully observed to obtain a clear picture of how power is used in the family, how decisions are made, and which members feel alienated and split off from the family system.

After the assessment process has been completed, the social worker and the family can begin to set out the goals of the treatment. The goals have a close relation to the assessment. The treatment plan is based upon a careful consideration of what will be effective in preventing future abuse and in providing a safe environment for the child. The social worker shares such decisions about goals with the parents to ensure their cooperation in working toward the desired outcomes.

Much effort should be made to state the goals in specific, concrete, behavioral terms. Vague and ambiguous statements such as "to be more loving" or to "improve communication" are not apt to be effective unless they are translated into behavioral terms for which the family can be called into account. The work of Blair and Rita Justice in stating goals is an excellent example of how this can be done in six areas of concern. The procedure involves the use of a Goal Attainment Scale that includes the following areas in which the family is having problems: (1) symbiosis, (2) isolation, (3) talking and sharing, (4) intemperance and temper, (5) child development and management, (6) employment. Parents determine what they plan to achieve in each of these areas within a three or six month period. For example, if a family has trouble with isolation, has no phone, makes no friends, and has no social contact, the goal might be to install a telephone, make two friends, and go out for some social event once per week (Justice & Justice, 1976, pp. 124-27). The social worker can determine if the home environment is safe by applying the goals-attainment scale. If the goals have been attained, the child can be returned to the care of the natural parents in those cases where custody has been given to someone outside the family. Or the families who have been caring for their children in their own homes can terminate treatment after the social worker has decided that the goals have been achieved.

Using Community Resources

Effective social work intervention in working with abusing families requires the use of various social and health services to meet special needs. The social worker must make these services available to the family and coordinate the work of the agencies involved in the best interest of the family. Among the auxiliary services that can be helpful are lay therapy, group therapy, crisis hot lines, crisis nurseries, family residential treatment and foster care.

Lay therapy. This is a service provided by parents who volunteer to provide emotional support for abusing parents by making frequent visits to the home. Lay therapists sometimes provide practical serv- vices such as transportation or helping the family deal with some problem needing immediate attention. Frequently the lay therapist (sometimes referred to as a parent aide) is able to establish a close friendship relation to the family. Experience shows that parents of the abused child feel free to talk to the parent aide about child-rearing problems in an informal manner. Lay therapists are carefully trained before assigned to work with abusing parents and are supervised by a professional staff member to ensure that they have someone to turn to when serious problems emerge.

Group therapy for parents. Social workers find that some abusing parents respond more positively to group therapy than to individual forms of treatment. The group experience provides an opportunity for the members to exchange points of view, to confront or to support each other. The group process can also be used to teach abusing parents facts about child development and child management that they can apply in dealing with problems of discipline and child- rearing. The effectiveness of Parents Anonymous as a self-help group illustrates the value of the group approach. The members of PA have access to a social network of persons available for help in times of crisis. Many abusing parents have an urgent need to talk with some- one when experiencing severe stress, and often feel comfortable in discussing their problems with other persons in similar situations.

Hot lines. Hot lines or telephone reassurance services provide a similar service for parents facing stress. These programs have been organized in many communities and are staffed with trained volunteers. Crisis nurseries have also been provided for parents to take their chil- dren to temporarily when they feel that they can no longer manage them and fear they might inflict injury. Many crisis nurseries are operated on a twenty-four hour basis so that they can provide prompt relief and assistance. The nursery staff also encourages abusing parents to seek professional help and assistance in dealing with their children.

Preschool for abused children. Preschool for abused children is an experimental form of group therapy for children between the ages of two and one half and five years of age. The purpose of preschools is to provide a respite for the parents, help the abused child over- come developmental lags, and expose the children to contacts with adults who treat them in nonviolent ways. The school staff consists of teachers especially trained in child development, assisted by paraprofessional aides. Experience with the preschool suggests most abused children will probably benefit from the individual attention given to each child who enters the school.

Family residential treatment. This form of help is designed to involve the entire family in a residential form of treatment. The family is admitted to the center along with the abused child, and normal family routine is carried out as much as possible. One parent goes to work while the other has major responsibility for the children's care, but both parents are required to participate in the treatment program at the center. The focus of treatment is on helping parents develop parenting skills and showing them how to interact with their children in new ways, reinforced by staff members who also model behavior for the parents to follow. Parents are invited to practice these techniques or to try to develop their own ways of interacting with their children. The center at Denver has been established as an alternative to separating the child from the parents and offering treatment that involves the father.

Public health services. Public health services can be very useful in working with abusing families. The public health nurse may be especially helpful to the social worker in obtaining the cooperation of the parents in carrying out a medical program so that physical problems receive adequate attention. Regular visits by a nurse can also help the parent learn to interact with the child in more constructive ways. The nurse can observe the way that the mother handles the child in dressing, feeding and bathing. As teacher and guide, the nurse can be a valuable aid in showing parents how to give better physical and emotional care to the abused child.

Foster care. Foster care is a temporary plan to protect the child if the risk of keeping the child in his parents' home is high. Foster care is usually not intended to serve as a permanent plan but as a way to buy time until careful study can be completed. There is danger in making a foster care plan if it is not monitored. The child may be left in limbo while agencies and courts try to decide about returning him to his natural parents' custody. In some cases, foster parents find the child troublesome; the usual solution is to change foster homes, and such frequent changes inflict further damage on the abused child. But abused children can often tax the patience of the best foster parents.

Group meetings under professional leadership can provide an opportunity for foster parents to discuss their difficulties and find solutions to the problems that abused children present.

The relation between the child's natural parents and foster parents is often strained and the child can be caught up in the hostility that develops. To prevent problems from becoming serious, the foster parents must not undermine the child's affection for his natural parents and should permit the natural parents to visit the foster home. Foster parents should also refrain from giving orders or advice to the child's own parents and also keep them informed about what is going on with the child. Because the task of foster parenting is a difficult one, special efforts should be made to give recognition to the important role they play in treating the abused child. The agency must extend to them the support and help needed to make foster care a useful experience for the child.

Case example. The effectiveness of working with the family and using community resources in helping abusing parents is illustrated in the following case.

Ann, the mother of two year old Tommy, admitted that she was responsible for injuries he had suffered. Angered by his refusal to eat his cereal one morning, she had jerked him out of his high chair and struck him repeatedly in the face, leaving severe bruises, a black eye, and bleeding from the mouth and nose. Shocked by what she had done, Ann called the crisis hot line for abusive parents, in a state of panic and remorse. "It was a matter of getting help or facing the awful possibility that this could happen again and the next time it might be too late," Ann told the social worker who answered her call.

The social worker assigned to investigate the matter assured the mother that every measure would be taken to help her so that incidents of violence would not be repeated. Ann felt quite relieved when she was informed that a medical examination showed that Tommy had sustained no permanent injury. Yet it was important for the social worker to find out what could have led to the abuse and to begin to find an answer to the problems causing family difficulties.

Ann told the social worker that there were times when she was quite depressed. She was not sure why, but on some days she just felt like staying in bed, not talking to anybody. She related that her husband, James, had been worried about his job as a construction worker. His boss had told him that there were no new construction contracts coming up and James had been laid off indefinitely. They were trying to make ends meet on the unemployment compensation check but were falling behind in paying their bills. Ann noticed that James was preoccupied and had begun to drink more than usual.

Ann wanted to talk about the problem, but James said there was no point to talking. Eventually Ann gave up trying to reach her husband. The relationship between them was beginning to deteriorate rapidly. Ann felt that her depression was primarily due to financial problems and to the effect James's inability to find work was having on the marriage.

Ann also said that she thought Tommy was a more difficult child than most. His whining and negative behavior irritated her. She had told James to give her a hand in managing Tommy, but it did not seem to work out. Tommy's father lost his temper with the boy and had often reached the point of inflicting serious harm on Tommy. Ann said that at first she had tried not to spank Tommy. She did shake him rather hard. Then she began to use a ping-pong paddle to get him to behave. On the morning in question she had really become extremely angry and had struck Tommy in the face with her hand four or five times in succession.

The social worker asked Ann what she would like to do about the situation. Did she have any ideas about what needed to be changed or how to go about it? Together Ann and the social worker began to set out some goals, among which were the following: (1) to be able to talk with James about their financial situation; (2) to work out a solution to paying the back bills; (3) to find some better way of managing Tommy's objectionable behavior. To accomplish these goals the social worker agreed to meet with James and Ann together to help them work out a solution to the financial problems. James was agreeable, and an appointment was set up for the following week. The interview with James and Ann resulted in a good exchange between them, something they had both wanted. They were now able to break through communication barriers.

The family service agency had recently started a consumer counseling program to help clients who had become involved in overextended buying on credit and who wanted to work out a plan that would be acceptable to the person to whom they owed money. The social worker put the couple in touch with the agency and a plan was put into place within two weeks. The financial strain was temporarily lifted, much to the relief of both James and Ann.

A program for abusing parents had also been recently established by Parents Anonymous. The group invited James and Ann to attend the weekly meetings. They accepted and now attend regularly. They have learned that other members of the group are also seriously trying to change their relationship to their children and Ann has made two new friends as a result of the contacts in PA.

The social worker is seeing Ann and James on a regular weekly basis to help them agree on ways to manage Tommy. They are now using the technique of "time out" to deal with his temper tantrums, this new approach seems to work out quite well. The social worker is also talking with James about his employment situation. He is planning to take a civil-service examination and has an interview for a maintenance job that is opening up in the next two weeks.

Ann and James are learning to talk over problems and work out a feasible, though not perfect, answer to some of the difficulties they encounter. As they told the social worker: facing things together makes them a lot easier.

Protective Services

Most states have established a program for the protection of battered children. Under these programs, all reports of child abuse are investigated by a specially designated agency. The child welfare division of the Department of Social Services is most often charged to study the circumstances surrounding the abuse, the family situation, and then report the findings in written form. In cases of serious abuse, the investigators also assume the obligation for filing petitions for the removal of the child from the home if there is evidence that the parents cannot provide a safe environment and if there is risk to the child's well-being.

The diagnosis and treatment of child abuse is often difficult to determine, especially in cases involving serious injury. In several communities, multidisciplinary child protection teams have been developed to carry out three important functions: (1) coordinating the efforts of all agencies involved in a given case; (2) sharing in decision-making about the disposition of cases; (3) developing guidelines for the uniform treatment of child-abuse cases. In regard to diagnosis, the team ensures that a comprehensive study has been made and works toward a consensus about the diagnosis and a treatment plan that will be effective in each specific situation. The team makes recommendations for intervention and also reviews the recommendations periodically. Treatment plans are revised in the light of new information. The team also coordinates and upgrades the services brought to bear on the child and his family. The focus is on rehabilitating the family and making the home a safe environment rather than terminating parental rights.

Members of the child protection team include a social worker, a physician, a nurse and a psychologist if possible. In addition to these, others may be asked to consult as needed. A member of a law enforcement agency familiar with the legal process is also added to help the team in matters of law. Treatment-review sessions are attended by the persons directly involved. Treatment-review provides the persons directly responsible for carrying out the treatment an opportunity to learn new skills through a discussion of the problems involved in working with abusing families. Treatment-review by the protection team also provides emotional support by sharing in decision-making in especially difficult or frustrating situations.

The protective service worker will inevitably come face to face with cases in which the separation of the child from the parents must be seriously considered. If the protection team is of the opinion that the child should be removed from home, a petition for custody of the child can be brought to the Juvenile Court by the Department of Social Welfare, together with a careful study and evaluation that set out the reasons why court action is required. The court hears evidence and is careful to consider the parents' rights before rendering a decision. The court usually considers four questions: How serious are the injuries inflicted on the child? Is there a history of past abuse? Are the parents willing to try to work out their problems? What are the possibilities of working with the parents towards a successful outcome?

In some courts, a *guardian ad litum* who represents the best interest of the child is appointed. The responsibility of the *guardian ad litum* is to see that the court has all the information needed to come to a reasonable decision in the best interest of the child and be aware of the individual needs of the specific case before the court. The *guardian ad litum* may make recommendations to the court at the close of the hearing. The cooperation of the child protection team, the *guardian ad litum* and the court can be a valuable aid in providing adequate protection for abused children and their families.

Preventive Measures

Social research and clinical experience provide a basis for understanding the causes of child abuse and designing measures to reduce the violence of parents against children. Steps that can be taken to accomplish this are early identification of high risk children, crisis intervention in cases of abuse, and parent education.

Early identification. Physicians and nurses are in an excellent position to observe the mother's reaction to the newborn baby. If at the end of three days the mother does not want to hold the baby, feed him and claim him as her own baby, there is strong reason to believe that this is a high risk case and requires careful study. The nurse can explore the mother's feelings about the baby, her notions of child-rearing. If she finds that there is some question about the care she will give the child, a wide variety of services can be offered. Frequent visits to a prenatal clinic or well-baby clinic provide an opportunity to help the parent understand infant behavior, to answer questions, to help the mother cope with problems and to give her emotional support during the crucial early months of the child's entry into the world. Public health nurses and school nurses are also in a strategic position to identify potential victims of abuse. Follow-up services in these cases may prevent the abuse from taking place.

Crisis intervention. The impact of crisis intervention has been found highly effective in helping people find new ways of coping with problems such as hospitalization of a mentally ill family member, incarceration of a delinquent child or loss of some important family member by reason of death, divorce or separation. Its techniques have been refined and are now available for application to cases of child abuse. The response, however, must be immediate and well planned to be effective. To this end, police officers, the most likely point of entry into violent family situations, need to be trained in how to proceed in cases of child abuse. Child welfare workers, in the front line of protecting children, must not only be adequately trained, but must have the time available to give the services that the family needs. Large caseloads prevent many child welfare workers from giving the necessary attention to adequately protect the child. Moreover, the family usually needs to have continuing service over an extended period in order to safeguard the child from further abuse. Too many familes do not receive continuing help and too often the child is again the victim of violence in the same home.

Parent education. The roots of child abuse can often be traced to the lack of any sound knowledge about child behavior and child development. The abusing parent often punishes the child for behavior seen as "bad," when it is really only normal for the child at a given age. Courses in parenting are now being offered in a number of communities. The introduction of programs that teach parenting skills in elementary and high schools is also a step in the right direction. This educational approach can be extended to abusing parents or to parents of "high-risk" children. Parent education can be carried out by carefully selected, well trained volunteers who can visit the home, establish a relationship of trust, and help the parents deal with problems of child management and discipline. Most abusing parents have only one form of discipline available to control the child's behavior, relying on force and physical punishment. They can benefit by being shown how to use nonviolent methods based upon principles of behavior modification that reinforce acceptable forms of conduct. Instruction by volunteers in these forms of nonviolent child management has been tried in several communities with excellent results.

The causes of child abuse are multidimensional and while the above measures are important parts of any attempt to deal with the problem, it is necessary to give attention to the social and cultural factors associated with child abuse. As Richard Gelles has stated; "The major flaw that exists in current programs and current strategies of intervention is that they amount to an ambulance at the bottom of a cliff. Child abuse programs are after the fact treatment of parents and children. What needs to be done is fix the road on the cliff that causes the accidents. Strategies would be developed that can deal with the problem before the child is beaten or killed" (Gelles, 1973, p. 621).

Social scientists have pointed out that our society encourages violence and that our culture sanctions the use of force against children. Children are subjected to mistreatment that would be regarded as criminal if an adult were the victim. As Gil points out, "Adult persons in American society have legal protection against physical attack by other persons. Children are not assured such protection" (Gil, 1971). Gil holds that children are denied equal protection under the law by this violation of the 14th Amendment to the U.S. Constitution. The culturally sanctioned use of force in child-rearing thus constitutes the basic level of all physical abuse of children.

The use of corporal punishment is a controversial issue for parents and teachers, with opinions strongly divided among those who favor and those who disapprove of it as a legitimate form of control. Extensive studies of family violence have come to the conclusion that use of corporal punishment is not productive. "Rarely, if ever," writes Gil, "is corporal punishment administered for the benefit of the attacked child; it usually serves the needs of the attacking adult seeking relief from anger and stress." In making recommendations for measures that would substantially reduce family violence, Strauss and his colleagues conclude that we must eliminate the norms that make the use of force against children legitimate: "As long as we, as a society, continue to believe that spanking children is necessary, good and beneficial to children; as long as we continue to believe that physical violence is an effective way to punish people; and as long as we accept violence as a means of solving problems and expressing one's self in the family and on the street, we will have a high level of violence in our homes and in our society" (p. 237).

Social scientists have also concluded that child abuse is associated with low income. Life in families surrounded by the grim reality of poverty face tremendous stress, one of the precursers of child abuse. The poor have very few ways of escaping stress. Accordingly, one of the ways of reducing the incidence of child abuse is to eliminate poverty. Reducing the hazards of unemployment, crowded housing, and unsafe neighborhoods is a beginning toward reducing stress. Unless we make a strong and determined effort to reduce the number of families living in poverty, we must accept the consequences of our indifference in terms of abuse toward children. Gil points out, "Abuse committed by society as a whole against large segments of the next generation through poverty, discrimination, malnutrition, poor housing and neighborhoods are...dangerous problems that merit the highest priority in the development of constructive social policies" (p. 238).

All studies on child abuse point to the unwanted child as the victim of family violence. Young mothers unready for marriage give birth to children who later become burdens on the young parents. Very young women become unwed mothers who find it difficult to meet the emotional and financial responsibilities involved in parenting. Babies are born into families already straining under the pressure to provide for three or four young children. The parents are not able to cope with the problems they already have in feeding and caring for their children. Family planning services made freely available, better education, and access to birth control devices and abortion on demand are necessary to prevent the problem of an unwanted child becoming the object of violence, mistreatment and injury.

Adequate health care is also an important preventive measure. Parents suffering from chronic and aggravating health problems are not capable of handling all the problems that arise in their families, and the possibility of a violent reaction to minor crisis situations increases the likelihood of injury to the child. The probability of mental illness is also a factor that needs to be taken into account in any prevention program. The pressure that parents experience makes inroads on their ability to function adequately. Early detection of symptoms that point to the need for mental health services in some member of the family and prompt attention to the problems is an important part of a comprehensive plan for preventing family violence.

Most of the abusing families that have been studied are known to be isolated and have few connections with a social network that can come to their assistance or sustain them during periods of difficulty. People who have friends to whom they can turn or who are part of an ongoing organization such as a church or club, are less likely to become violent. Modern life tends to increase the possibility of social isolation because of frequent moves, re-locating families every two or three years and preventing the possibility of putting down roots in the new community. Old neigh-borhoods are sometimes destroyed by the construction of a super-highway, breaking up the ties between people that are the life blood of the community. Families are displaced and forced into living conditions not of their choice. Family disruption is associ-ated with an unstable environment, the result is violence. Therefore, an effective way to prevent family violence must encourage the for-mation of social networks that give stability and support to families, integrating them into a larger system of kinship and community relationships.

Finally, the cycle of violence transmitted from one generation to the next must be broken. All studies of child abuse point out that using violence against children is a learned pattern of be-havior. Adults who have not grown up in a violent family do not generally become physically abusive toward their children. Abusing parents have usually themselves been abused as children. Men who beat their wives have seen their own parents inflict injury on one another. Unless this cycle of violence is broken, the possibility of reducing the number of abused children will re-main in doubt. The notion that physical punishment is necessary and good must be replaced by the notion that the use of physical aggression against children in any form is wrong and harmful. There are effective nonviolent alternatives for raising children with-out the use of force. The training of parents in these methods is essential to break the repetition of child abuse. By so doing we can prevent children from learning to use violence on those they love.

References

Gil, D. A socio-cultural perspective on child abuse. *Child Welfare,* 1971, *50*, 7.

Gelles, R. Child abuse as psychopathology. *American Journal of Orthopsychiatry,* 1973, *43*, 621.

Justice, B. & Justice, R. *The abusing family.* New York: Human Sciences Press, 1976.

Martin, H. P. *The abused child.* Cambridge, Mass.: Ballinger Publishing, 1976. *New Hampshire Times,* February 12, 1974.

Strauss, M., Gelles, R., & Steinmetz, Şusanne. *Behind closed doors.* Garden City, N.Y.: Anchor Press, 1980.

Thorman, G. *Family violence.* Springfield, Ill.: Charles C. Thomas, 1980.

SEVEN

Acquiring Skills

Effective intervention in dysfunctional family systems is based upon social work principles in working with individuals, families and groups. Graduate social work education provides the practitioner with this knowledge base. Continuing education programs sponsored by universities and training centers provide opportunities for social workers to build upon this base by participating in seminars, workshops and training programs that teach the special skills needed to practice behavioral social work, family therapy, and network intervention. A combination of classroom teaching and practicum experience under close supervision enables social workers to become proficient in using these three models of intervention with disordered and troubled families.

Behavioral Social Work Training
Learning to apply the behavioral approach in intervention begins with a knowledge of the social learning theories that underlie this model of social work practice. This content is usually taught in seminars that deal with the application of learning theory to human development, personality formation, and social functioning. The emphasis is on behavioral assessment. Students are trained to identify those antecedent conditions and consequences that produced the undesired behavior and to assess the environmental forces that maintain it. A major goal is to enable the trainees to see the relationship between learning theory and the use of behavior modification techniques.

Seminars teaching theory are accompanied by a supervised laboratory practicum. The trainees are required to demonstrate their competence in applying theory to actual practice. The content of the seminars includes a knowledge of the operant respondent and modeling paradigms for intervention with children and adults. The seminars also enable trainees to become proficient in making clinical assessments, identifying target behaviors, various treatment interventions, and the choice of appropriate techniques to effect behavioral change.

Wodarski and Bagarozzi have outlined a curriculum in behavioral social work combining theory with supervised experience. In the early stages, students, are expected to treat at least one case, using the behavioral approach (Wodarski and Bagarozzi, 1980, p. 275). They are also required to present a written report describing how the approach was used and the effectiveness of treatment. The trainees are expected to be competent in making an accurate assessment of the presenting problem, including a statement of the problem in specific behavioral terms, the conditions that precede or follow the problem behavior, and the reinforcing events that maintain the behavior.

Trainees are also required to set forth a specific behavioral statement of treatment goals, identifying the behaviors to be increased, the behaviors to be decreased, and new behaviors to be acquired as a result of the treatment. Trainees also set forth a treatment plan that clearly states what techniques will be used and the rationale for choosing these modification techniques. The treatment plan also specifies the means of intervention, that is, individual, group, or family, as well a list of the techniques to be used. In addition, the treatment plan indicates who will carry out the behavior modification regime, where it will be carried out, and how the treatment is to be monitored.

The clinical practicum experience is designed to provide an opportunity for trainees to learn through experience in a highly structured and closely supervised program requiring a considerable amount of time and effort. Trainees observe a variety of behaviors involving different clients and situations. During the course of their work, the trainees are expected to master a variety of behavior modification techniques; corrective feedback is given to the trainees through the use of audiovisual tape recordings, observation by trained behavioral raters, and other forms of evaluation.

Demonstrations of behavioral social work by experienced practitioners and faculty are an excellent learning procedure, as are roleplaying of simulated cases and videotape recordings illustrating the use of specific forms of intervention. Use of a one-way mirror where trainees can observe instructors conduct interviews with clients and families is also a very valuable teaching device.

Specific educational goals for the practicum experience are set out so that the trainee will gain experience in all phases of the treatment process. Among the experiences included in the practicum are assessing the problematic behavior identified by the client, or the client's family, applying a variety of techniques in changing problematic behavior, and evaluating the outcome of the treatment. Agencies that want to develop staff members competent to use behavioral social work techniques will also need to be prepared to provide training facilities such as videotapes, one-way mirrors, and procedures for expert evaluation and feedback that will enable the practitioner to enhance his performance. Incentives must also be provided for staff to attend conferences and workshops to keep abreast of the new developments in the field.

Training in Network Intervention

Using the network intervention approach in working with family problems requires the social worker to become familiar with the principles that underlie networking and to acquire its special skills. Uri Rueveni, a psychologist at Eastern Pennsylvania Psychiatric Institute, has developed a training program that includes an introduction to social network intervention, an advanced seminar that prepares trainees for practice, and an on-site consultation and training designed to help trainees adapt network intervention to their own specific needs (Rueveni, 1979).

The introductory seminar is conducted once a week for ten weeks. It intends to familiarize trainees with the criteria for selecting families, the phases of the networking process and the techniques used in the procedure. The training program presents theoretical material and experimental components designed to achieve these goals.

One component requires the trainees to explore their own family and social networks. Each trainee meets with other trainees to discuss family relationships and friendships. In small support groups, they share their findings and explore the value of network systems in their own lives and their usefulness as resources in time of need. This personal sharing among support-group members provides a learning experience that leads to a better understanding of the networking process in helping families cope in crisis situations. These support groups continue throughout the ten week training seminar.

Simulated home visits and networking sessions are also used extensively during the training course. Simulated home visits are developed by the staff, allowing the trainees to play both family and intervention-team members. As team members, the trainees interview a family facing a severe crisis outlined by the staff. They discuss the nature of the problem with the simulated family, inquire into efforts the family has made in the past to resolve the problem, and prepare the family for network intervention. Following the simulated home visits, trainees are asked to discuss the experience of playing a family or team member. They are also given an opportunity to question the work of the team and give feedback that will enhance the trainees' ability to use networking techniques more effectively.

Simulated networking intervention sessions are also included in the training seminar. The staff can assign family member roles or the trainees can assemble the family by choosing among group members and defining the role each trainee is to play in the simulated session. The nature of the crisis is explained to those involved in the family network. The training staff and selected trainees act as the intervention team. The intervention session is videotaped and after the simulation has been completed, the staff and trainees view the session on the monitor. Videotape recordings provide trainees an opportunity to become familiar with a variety of situations frequently found in practice. The staff and trainees also become acquainted with various techniques and their appropriate application in given situations, ask questions, and make observations about the work of the intervention team.

An advanced training seminar is offered to trainees who have completed the introductory seminar to prepare trainees for actual practice in their own settings. The advanced seminars meet biweekly and include theoretical material and research aspects. Trainees discuss the work they are performing in their own settings and receive the benefit of group feedback and the observations of the training staff. The training staff is also available for on-site consultation and training, involving the personnel of the agency in learning how to use network intervention in cases brought to their attention. The on-site consultation can result in the formation of small support groups within the agency and these groups usually form the basis for the development of an intervention team.

Videotape recordings are used extensively in the training program. Each videotape focuses on some special aspect of networking and some videotape sessions focus on a specific form of dysfunctioning. One videotape presents a depressed woman with her family and demonstrates how the team mobilizes the support of her husband and her two children to help her cope with her depression. Other taped sessions focus on issues of family members' separation from home, family or spouse. The use of network intervention in modifying self-destructive symbiotic ties is demonstrated in helping a mother and her psychotic son cut their mutually destructive bonds. Network intervention with a suicidal family member presents the process of helping the extended family system prevent a suicide. Videotapes are also used to demonstrate the use of networking in mobilizing the family system to help a drug-abusing family member. The videotape presentations are followed by a group discussion during which trainees can ask questions or discuss issues raised in the recorded session.

Training in Family Therapy

The development of family therapy has led to a variety of programs specifically designed to train students and beginning practitioners. Universities offer graduate courses in the theory of family therapy. Workshops and continuing education programs sponsored by mental health centers in various parts of the country offer opportunities for both beginning and experienced therapists to explore new techniques that will enrich their practice. Clinical centers provide special training under experienced family therapists. Videotape is being used as a learning medium and provides new, more effective methods of training and supervision. Films and videotape recordings produced by prominent family therapists are avialable to demonstrate various styles of therapy, different approaches, and special techniques.

Family therapy begins with teaching the student or beginning practitioner to gather information about certain patterns of interaction that create and maintain family pathology. Several tests and instruments are available to teach family diagnostic procedures systematically, among them the Timberlawn Scale described in Chapter Two, developed by Lewis and his associates (Lewis, 1976). This scale is especially useful as a frame of reference for beginning students because its variables focus on areas of family functioning: how power is distributed, how relationships among family members are structured, and how communication is used in negotiation. If students arrive at a clear understanding of these variables, they can learn to apply them by viewing a segment of videotape that records a brief example of family interaction. After viewing the television segment, students make an analysis of the information it provides, using the scale as a guide to arrive at judgments. The scale is an instrument that forces students to give attention to specific areas of functioning and enables observation of each distinct variable of the family system. Repeated use of the scale by students and discussion of how judgments are reached helps students make rapid gains in arriving at a family diagnosis.

Other approaches to testing have also been developed to aid therapists in the diagnostic procedure. These tests can be used to teach students to observe the family in the performance of a given task, such as planning a picnic or working out a menu for a meal. Such "tests" can be easily administered by the student and do not require complicated equipment. An audio tape recorder is all that is needed to record the family interaction. A videotape recording is desirable, but not essential, to obtain a sample of how the family members communicate and how they relate in performing a given task. The family is given general instructions. For example: "I would like you to plan a picnic as a family. You can talk among yourselves and decide what you would do, where you would go and other things that are involved in carrying out the plans. You have ten minutes to complete making your plans. I will leave the room, and at the end of that time, I will return. I would like to have your permission to record your discussion on this tape recorder." The student and supervising staff member listen to the tape recording together. The recording is stopped at crucial points during the replay so that the supervisor can ask for comments from the student. The supervisor also comments, indicating what is particularly relevant to understanding how the family functions.

As part of their training, students can be asked to participate in an informal staff discussion of a family in the beginning phase of therapy. Brief segments of a videotape recording of the family session are selected for viewing. Students are then asked to make an assessment of the family based on what they have seen and heard. The supervisor can ask the students to use a diagnostic guide to help them look for certain information. Brief segments of tape, lasting from three to five minutes, are the most useful, because trainees can become confused and overwhelmed viewing an entire family session when beginning their orientation to diagnosis: attention to the details of family interaction is difficult to sustain over a longer time. Group discussion of the videotape enables the trainee to make comprehensive and accurate assessments of family systems, especially if the learning experience is frequently repeated.

Structured simulations in which trainees are given a script describing the family situation in broad outline, are also useful. Students act out the family roles set forth in the script. The student assuming the role of therapist does not have advance knowlege of what is contained in the script. The instructor sets a limit of ten minutes for the role-playing.

After the script has been acted out, the family members are asked to comment on the session, and the instructor elicits their responses regarding family roles, relationships, communication, and conflict resolution. The observers compare their assessment with that of the students involved in the role-playing, so that similarities and differences in points of view emerge in formulating the family diagnosis.

After the diagnostic assessment has been discussed, the student playing the therapist describes what direction therapy would take were work to be continued with the family. The observers outline the goals of therapy and the discussion revolves around similarities and differences in points of view about treatment plans and intervention goals.

The supervisor or instructor may use the structured simulation to present a variety of learning experiences. For example, the Timberlawn scale of crucial variables may be used as a guide to assessing family functioning to teach students what to observe and to help them formulate a family diagnosis. Or the simulated family therapy session may be recorded and used as a medium for teaching students some particular aspect of family interaction and family dynamics.

Teaching Aids

Family sculpting. This technique can be used to help beginning therapists to understand, and come to terms with, their own family as an aid to understanding their client families (Duhl, 1974). In family sculpting, a trainee is asked to depict his or her own family at a certain point in time. The trainee chooses people in the group to play the roles of parents and siblings. Each player is asked to assume a certain relation to other family members, with the trainee deciding where each family member is to stand and what bodily posture in to be assumed. For example, the father may be placed opposite or adjacent to the mother. The mother may face the father or may turn away from him and face one of the children. Children can be grouped in a cluster or separated by considerable distance. One child may be placed in close proximity to the mother, another close to the father. The trainee places him or herself in the family scene after the family has been sculpted satisfactorily.

The actors who assume the role of the family members are then asked how they feel in relation to other family members. In turn, each student comments about his or her position in the family. Some indicate that they feel ''isolated'' or ''left out'' while other family members respond that they feel ''smothered'' or ''hemmed in.'' Still others express satisfaction because they are protected by other family members or because they have a privileged position within the family system.

The experience of sculpting can serve as a useful device by providing a dramatic portrayal of family relationships. Splits and alignments within the family can be identified by the distance between family members. Not only does the main participant learn a great deal about his or her own family situation by examining the meaning of what has been sculpted. Others involved in the scuplting also feel a deep relevance to their own family situations and may benefit as much as the main participant. The sculpting technique is highly useful and effective as a method of teaching how relationships are formed within the family system.

Interpersonal Process Recall. Kagan developed Interpersonal Recall as a technique for educating beginning practitioners in family therapy. The trainee is asked to view a monitor during a playback of his or her own family session. The tape is stopped at a given point and the supervisor asks questions such as, "Can you tell me what you felt at this point?" Or "What did it mean when the client frowned?" The purpose is to encourage the trainees to make a detailed analysis of the interaction with a given client by exploring the experience in depth and recalling the meaning of the interaction.

This use of the IPR technique led to another phase in training. The trainee's interview was videotaped, and then played back in the presence of the client and the trainee, with the supervisor joining them. All three persons participated in a discussion of the interview, with the supervisor asking pertinent questions. During the first part of the recall session, the supervisor only asked questions of the client, exploring the client's reaction at particular points in the interaction. The supervisor then asked the trainee to respond to what the client said and to comment on his or her own feelings and thoughts about the interaction. By repeating this process, the trainee became aware of how this communication and behavior affected the course of the interaction between him or herself and the client.

Videotape Simulation. Another technique in the training of students is videotape simulation which consists of a combination of role-playing by the trainees and the use of television equipment to record the role-playing scene. Each player is given a brief statement of the problem to be presented. Some trainees are assigned roles as family members. One is assigned the role of family therapist. No script is provided. The supervisor or teacher acts as director and asks the players to play out the scene. The actors may be asked to exchange roles, for example, from the role of father to brother, or from son to therapist. The recorded sessions usually run from twenty to thirty minutes.

The simulated role-playing is then presented to the class for discussion. Students may interrupt the videotape at any time to comment or question. This continues throughout the playing of the tape. Froelich, who has used videotape simulation in the training of medical students is enthusiastic about the results. He reports that students become totally involved in their reenactments. "All our videotape sessions have been filled with affect," he reports. "The role-players have become involved in the situation and have expressed frustration, anger, denial and other feelings common to the roles they were playing" (Froelich, 1970). He points out that students learn best by being able to "dig for themselves," by acting out problems they will confront in later life and practice. He believes that coupling problem-solving activity with theory leads to a greater retention of knowledge and results in better learning.

My own experience in teaching courses in family therapy bears out these conclusions. Students find the enactment of simulated problem situations to be an effective way to learn the practice of therapy and to apply theory to a variety of problems.

A combination of the IPR procedure and simulated role-playing can be an effective teaching medium. Students are instructed to concentrate attention on the communication patterns within the family, noting how the therapist attempts to alter and improve the communication process during the course of the simulated interview. Five students may participate in role-playing, with four assuming the role of family members (two parents and two children) and one assuming the role of the therapist. Students who play family members identify who they are and briefly describe the problem that brings them to family therapy. Identifying material such as age, occupation, and race is supplied, but no script is provided. Given these bare essentials, the students begin the simulated family interview. The remaining students form a circle around the role-players and act as observers, taking notes on the interaction process.

The discussion that follows the role-playing begins with the teacher asking family members to react to what happened during the session, with special attention to what was helpful and what was not helpful. The teacher guides the students to examine interaction between therapist and family members in detail. The student playing the therapist is then asked to respond to the comments of the family, again analyzing the interaction in depth under the guidance and inter-rogation of the instructor. Finally, the observers are invited to discuss the observations they have made and comment on strengths or weak-nesses they saw in the work of the student therapist.

Variations can be developed to accomplish different purposes. The role-players may be assigned to enact a situation typical of a certain client population with special problems such as an older parent, a rebelling teenager, or an abusing family situation. By enacting a wide variety of situations, students learn how to use the family approach to help solve problems that may at first glance seem to be unresponsive to family therapy. Role-playing can be so structured as to involve other considerations such as social class, ethnic back-ground, or race. Within this context, the students are made aware of the significance of class and culture in determining how therapy can accommodate the values and lifestyle of a family not identified with predominant social norms.

The simulated family therapy session can also be used by the supervisor or instructor to demonstrate special aspects of therapy. In this case, the instructor can play the therapist, with the students form-ing a simulated family. Students usually prefer that the instructor "model" a family therapy session in the classroom before they them-selves attempt role-playing as family therapists. In acting as therapist to the simulated family, the instructor can give direction to the inter-view and structure the learning experience.

When a student has difficulty working with the simulated family, the instructor may wish to "spontaneously" enter into the role-playing situation. Such active intervention may take the form of "live supervi-sion." A student may be given suggestions as to how to deal with an impasse, change direction, or ask for information in a different way. In some cases, the student therapist or the students in the family are in-terrupted to ascertain how they view the situation that has led to a "dead end" so that they can immediately analyze the therapeutic problem.

The simulated family interview has a special value in preparing students for their first "real" interview. The experience in a rehearsal enables them to engage in their first family interview with a little more confidence than if they had never had an opportunity to work with a simulated family under controlled conditions.

Training and Co-therapy. Family therapy offers the possibility of the use of a co-therapist as an effective method of training beginning practitioners and students. An experienced therapist who invites an inexperienced practitioner to join in the treatment of a family opens opportunities to learn seldom found in individual psychotherapy. The exposure of ignorance is not devastating to the inexperienced therapist working with a co-therapist who can assume control when help is needed. Moreover, the trainee can take a passive role during the sessions in the beginning phases. The student can sit in on family sessions as an observer until a level of confidence is achieved that enables more active participation. The family involved seldom has any marked discomfort in the presence of a new therapist just beginning "to learn the ropes."

My own experience as a co-therapist wth a beginning therapist has convinced me that this is usually the most effective way to teach because of the close interaction between co-therapists during the training process. Each session with the family is followed by a debriefing between the trainer and the trainee, leading to a clearer understanding of family dynamics and intervention techniques. Abstract theories and concepts become real and useful, discussed in relation to a specific family. The trainee develops a sense of responsibility in making judgments, suggesting possible changes in the direction of treatment, or the use of special techniques. As skills develop, the inexperienced therapist can begin to take the initiative during family sessions, testing his or her ability to assume a more active role in the treatment process.

The team experience provides an opportunity for learning through participation that is more meaningful than the traditional methods of teaching and supervision. Learning by doing therapy is more effective than reading about therapy. By the same token, learning by doing therapy with another therapist as a partner, is often more effective than working alone. As Haley has observed, therapy is a personal encounter. "It cannot be learned by watching others do it, although watching is valuable at certain points in training. Therapy is a personal encounter and a therapist can only learn how to do it by doing it. All other training activity is peripheral, if not irrelevant" (Haley, 1976, p. 181).

Training Through Supervision

Group supervision. This method of training has several advantages over individual supervison. It is more economical and exposes the students to a larger number of cases in a shorter period of time. If eight students observe four cases from behind a one-way mirror, thirty-two cases have been presented. Moreover, the supervisor can watch the students doing therapy behind a one-way mirror and provide constructive comments, allowing the group to learn as the interview is in progress.

Group supervision also encourages the expression of ideas about what to do with the family under discussion. The student conducting a therapy session not only has input from the supervisor, but can benefit from the contributions of peers. When students have problems with difficult cases, the group provides helpful support.

Group supervision also helps students think through what they are doing in therapy and arrive at a rational and coherent basis for their work. Students can present videotapes of their work to one another and to the supervisor, commenting as to why a certain course of action was selected. By explaining these decisions to others, the student begins to examine this performance more critically and becomes increasingly articulate in expressing ideas about family therapy.

The group discussions that involve the students' work with a family helps trainees integrate what whey have learned about theory with actual practice. Special reading assignments that relate directly to some special problem that emerges from review of the tape-recorded session will enable trainees to investigate the family therapy literature and widen their knowledge. For example, the trainee may attempt to invole the family in the performance of a task, but have difficuly in selecting an appropriate task relating to the problem they are trying to solve. The supervisor can suggest readings that describe how the therapist selects a task and how the family is engaged in carrying it out.

Haley has noted that students need to learn how to give directives to the family. This is especially important if the trainee undertakes the use of a task-centered approach in working with the family. Clinicians trained in traditional therapy methods receive little or no instruction in giving directives. "A training program in directive therapy must include teaching students how to motivate someone to do what he is told; how to give directives, how to clarify whether they have been understood, how to anticipate reluctance to follow them, and how to check to see if they have been followed" (Haley, 1976, p. 184).

In group supervision, the students can offer suggestions as to how a task could have been planned in the specific case that has been reviewed. Alternate ways of structuring the task can be explored in the group discussion and the trainee can gain knowledge from the contribution peers make in a specific area of practice. In the process, students also learn to appraise their work in terms of their strong points and areas in which their skills need to be improved. They also gain psychological support in finding that other members of the group also have difficulty in certain areas and that they can share their frustrations and their pride in achievement with other trainees.

Group supervision is also useful in teaching students to evaluate their work by requiring students to inquire into how the family deals with problems after termination. Students can be taught to use follow-up interviews with their families. By giving special attention to the outcome of treatment, the trainee is taught to focus attention on change as the measure of therapeutic effectiveness. "Focusing on outcome forces the therapist to orient toward change," writes Haley (p. 186). In the process of reviewing and evaluating therapeutic activity by engaging the family in follow-up interviews, the trainee learns to direct efforts to identifying the problems that need to be solved and to help the family manage to solve future problems without such help. If these efforts have not been successful in effecting the desired change, the trainee is taught to think of ways in which the therapy could have been more effective, what procedures might have been used to help the family solve problems, and how his or her techniques could have been improved. This follow-up procedure makes the student aware of how therapy should be modified in working with other families in similar situations.

Supervision with videotape recording. This method offers a revolutionary change in teaching family therapy. In the past, the supervisor seldom saw the family and felt no genuine sense of what the family was like except through the trainee's reports at supervisory conferences. These reports carried a high degree of subjectivity, if not down-right inaccuracy, and left the supervisors uncertain about the quality of the trainee's work. Videotape has changed this; the supervisor is no longer in the dark, and has an opportunity to see the trainee in action with the family. The Department of Psychiatry at the UCLA School of Medicine has used this method of supervision in training residents in psychiatry with much success. The staff report that the supervisor, in effect, becomes a co-therapist to the resident, assuring that the therapy is properly carried out and benefits the family. The use of videotape recording changes the relation between the resident and the supervisor in an important respect. Although every recorded session is not viewed, the supervisor is in much better touch with the family and with the trainee. "A supervisor more in touch makes for a more comfortable and honest relationship between himself and the resident," Gruenberg reports (1970, p. 52). Supervisors are aware of certain resident's needs to impress them by presenting fabrications. With videotape, all that can be removed.

Videotape recording of the trainees' interviews enables the supervisor to call attention to certain recorded transactions of which the trainee is not aware. For example, nonverbal behavior in the interview is an important factor in therapy. The trainee and the supervisor can identify the significance of nonverbal interactions which could not be discovered in any other way. Moreover, trainees often do not recognize opportunities for appropriate intervention at strategic points in a family session. Similarly, the supervisor can become aware of what might have otherwise been missed by seeing the resident as he or she actually works with the family. By viewing the videotape in the presence of the supervisor, the student becomes aware of what to observe and begins to monitor these recorded sessions without the supervisor's presence.

At UCLA the videotapes serve an additional purpose. From time to time, visiting consultants are invited to discuss topics of special interest. They are also invited to view videotape recordings of family therapy sessions. Consultants focus attention on aspects of treatment overlooked or not emphasized by the supervisor. While residents feel some uneasiness when their work is subjected to public exposure, there is a payoff in learning. The first exposure of this kind can cause a great deal of anxiety, and sometimes students beg off from having sessions recorded. In most cases, however, this initial anxiety begins to dissipate as students view the recordings of their peers and find their own performances to be as good or even better than others'. In the end, the students often ask to have extra time allotted to detailed study of their tape recordings so that they can learn to observe more closely and improve their level of competence.

There is some reason to believe that the taping of sessions actually improves trainee performance, as indicated at UCLA. For some time, recording facilities were temporarily not in use, and one resident began to see patients in his office. When the interviews were not being recorded on videotape, both the resident and the patients expressed the opinion that therapy seemed to be slowing down. After a two month interval, the patient and the resident moved back into the televison recording room and resumed taping the sessions. The tempo and effectiveness of therapy showed marked improvement. "This indicates that the cessation and subsequent resumption of videotaping were clearly related to the effectiveness of therapeutic activity. Succinctly stated, when one is under intense scrutiny, whether it be in psychotherapy or surgery, it is reasonable to expect a more intense investment of attention to the problem at hand''(p. 53).

Live Supervision. Closed circuit television now makes it possible for the supervisor to observe the student in the process of working with the family as it occurs. The supervisor monitors the screen and can intervene by sending messages to the student during the therapy session. The supervisor can send messages by phone or convey them by the ''bug in the ear'' device often used on commercial television. Haley is of the opinion that the telephone is a better way to convey messages because the supervisor will not interrupt as often if the phone must be used. In a given call, the supervisor presents only one idea, because it is difficult for a therapist to remember a series of suggestions in the process of working with a family. Such suggestions should be stated as briefly as possible. If the suggestion is quite involved, the student may need more clarification, in which case a graceful departure from the room to discuss the issue with the supervisor is indicated.

The use of live supervision by video monitor is not a substitute for the long-term supervision needed to give continuity to the therapeutic process. The general strategy and techniques employed in therapy can be discussed before the interview, and are not matters that can be dealt with easily in live supervison. Haley points out that ''What is crucial during live supervison is brief interventions by the supervisor that make the interview go well and also teach the student some aspect of therapeutic skill'' (Haley, 1976, p. 193). Haley also believes that the supervisor and the therapist should agree that any suggestion is *only* a suggestion because the supervisor is not completely aware of what is happening and can miss many empathetic aspects of the interview that only the therapist and the family can fully appreciate.

Students sometimes feel that the family will be uncomfortable if they know that the session is being recorded. Such is seldom the case, and families usually welcome the recording without objection. In most cases, the student is the one who is uncomfortable, and often any concern about the family is a reflection of his or her own anxiety. In any case, the family should know that the session is being recorded; permission to proceed with the videotape must be obtained in all situations. The family should also have the proper assurance of privacy in the use of the videotape recordings, with constant emphasis on the need to safeguard the integrity of consenting families (Rosenbaum, 1970).

Jay Haley summarized the advantages of live supervision and the opportunities that videotape recording opens for training in family therapy:

> We have progressed, over the last twenty years, from a supervisory model in which a student made notes and took them to a supervisor who tried to guess what happened from those comments. After that, we had audio tapes so that a supervisor could at least know what was said. Then came videotapes, so that both the words and the movement could be observed and commented on. Yet in none of those procedures could there be any help and guidance at the time the student needed it most—when he was in the act of interviewing. With live supervision we finally are able to teach how to do therapy at the moment when the therapist is doing just that (p. 194).

Centers for Training

Centers that offer training in family therapy are sometimes difficult to find. Most training in psychotherapy takes place in institutions and hospitals seldom geared to family therapy training. Inpatient settings have several disadvantages. They often place most of the emphasis in teaching diagnosis and on the effects of different psychotropic medications. Moreover, since the patient's family may live in a distant city, involving them in therapy becomes problematic. Under these conditions, obtaining training in the technqiues of family therapy becomes difficult. Therefore, students should seek out possibilities for working in community mental health clinics and psychiatric out-patient service centers where they can have access to the family and can gain experience in using a family approach to the solution of a wide range of problems.

Child guidance centers and family service agencies frequently offer an excellent opportunity to learn about and engage in family therapy. An outstanding example is the Jewish Family Service agency in New York City that began to develop family therapy practice in the late 1950's under the direction of Ackerman and Sanford. Another example is the Philadelphia Child Guidance Center where Minuchin, Haley, Montalvo and other staff members are involved in training family therapists. Because these agencies are the sources to which many people are referred for help with family problems, marital difficulties and parent-child relationship problems, they are able to offer family therapy as a major form of counseling and treatment.

In choosing a place for training, the nature and quality of the supervision should be uppermost in the mind of the student or prospective practitioner. The training center should have facilities such as one-way mirrors or television recording that the student and supervisor use consistently during the training. The supervisor should observe the student during sessions with the family and give live supervision so that the student will be carefully guided while doing therapy. Videotaping of student sessions should be done routinely to provide for student review and discussion in considerable detail with the supervisor.

Most family service agencies, child guidance clinics, and mental health centers offer students opportunities to work with a variety of problems and types of clients. Students learn to deal with children, young people, couples, and older persons. Most agencies also serve a wide range of different populations, including lower-class, middle-class and upper-class clients. Students therefore learn to deal with issues and problems of special concern to these clients. The variety of problems found in families that use these services also maximizes the flexibility of the student so that s/he feels comfortable with many different situations. Students trained in these centers can also develop an ability to work in different contexts, such as therapy in the home, the school, and the neighborhood, as well as in the office.

A number of excellent workshops are offered each year by well-known training centers. These workshops provide a rare opportunity for practitioners to receive intensive short-term training under an expert family therapist. These workshops are usually held for only two days, but a brief concentrated period of training has great value in helping students and beginning practitioners develop skills. Universities offer programs in continuing education that include formal courses in family therapy during the summer session. Courses are held over a period of ten days or two weeks and are the equivalent of a full semester of three credit hours. Seminars, workshops and postgraduate courses are highly useful programs that increase the effectiveness of beginning social work practitioners in working with troubled families.

The literature on family therapy is rapidly expanding. A variety of approaches is being developed to enrich the practice of family therapy. Researchers inquiring into the dynamics of family systems are discovering important information for those engaged in helping troubled families. Social workers have always been in the forefront of efforts to strengthen the family. As we learn more about the techniques of intervention, social workers will undoubtedly find more effective ways to carry out the traditional mission of helping families in times of crisis.

References_____

Duhl, E. Learning, space and action in family therapy. In D. Bloch
(Ed.), *Techniques of family therapy*. New York: Grune and
Stratton, 1974.

Froelich, R. Teaching psychotherapy to medical students through
videotape simulation. In M. Berger, (Ed.), *Videotape in psychiatric training and treatment*. New York: Brunner/Mazel, 1970.

Gruenberg P. Intensive supervison of psychotherapy with videotape
recordings. In M. Berger, (Ed.),*Videotape in psychiatric training
and treatment*. New York: Brunner/Mazel, 1970.

Haley, J. *Problem solving therapy*. San Francisco: Jossey Bass, 1976.

Haley, J. *Changing families*. New York: Grune and Stratton, 1971.

Kagan, N. Television in counselor supervision. In M. Berger, (Ed.),
Videotape in psychiatric training and treatment. New York:
Brunner/Mazel, 1970.

Lewis, J. M. *No single thread: Psychological health in family systems*. New York: Brunner/Mazel, 1976. ˙

Rosenbaum, M. The issues of privacy and privileged communication. In M. Berger, (Ed.), *Videotape in psychiatric training and
treatment*. New York: Brunner/Mazel, 1970.

Rueveni, Uri. *Networking families in crisis*. New York: Human
Sciences Press, 1979.

Wodarski, J. and Bagarozzi, D. *Behavioral social work*. New York:
Human Sciences Press,1980.

EIGHT

Applying Theories Relevant to Practice

Helping troubled families solve problems requires the intelligent application of theories about human behavior and the social environment to social work practice. Among the theoretical orientations especially relevant and useful in working with families are: systems theory, role theory, communication theory and social learning theory. Each of these orientations to human behavior and the psychodynamics of the family has important implications for how the social worker assesses family problems, sets goals for intervention and defines his or her role in the helping process.

Systems Theory

Systems theory provides the worker with a conceptual framework that shifts attention from the individual and his characteristics to the interactions that occur within the family system. The systems approach allows us to study the family as a unit by focusing on the processes that take place as family members interact with and react to one another. The family is viewed as a microsocial system in which individuals carry out certain roles essential to the proper functioning of the system in maintaining its viability. All systems also strive to achieve a state of homeostasis, that is, a degree of equilibrium and stability in order to accommodate to changes within the family system itself or to changes in the social environment. If one part of the system is changed in some respect, the family tries to accommodate by establishing a state of equilibrium that takes such change into account.

If the father becomes disabled, the mother may take over the role of wage earner and provider in order to keep the family intact. Other family members will also accommodate to the changed situation. Children will take over some of the funtions that the mother is no longer able to carry out.

The application of systems theory is also useful in making us aware how relationships among family members are structured. In any social system, individuals occupy a position within a hierarchy. Family members also occupy a position in relation to other members. The family develops a power structure of its own that distributes power among its members in a fairly well defined pattern or "pecking order." The system approach to studying a family unit also enables the worker to arrive at conclusions about alignments and splits within the family system. On the basis of his observations, the worker can then determine whether a particular family structure is creating difficulties for the family. For example, a weak coalition between the parents may be creating and maintaining a high level of conflict or chaos in the family system. Or a highly symbiotic tie between the mother and the son may obstruct the development of his autonomy and arrest his maturation processes.

One important principle underlying systems theory is that any given system is in a continuous process of interaction with other systems. From this point of view, a family system is seen within a broad context that calls attention to systems outside the family itself that have a significant impact on the way it functions. The family system interfaces with a social and physical environment made up of other systems: the school system, the governmental system, the economic system and other subsystems. Each of these systems in turn has its own structure. The school system consists of the school board, the chief administrators, principals and teachers, all of whom have a certain authority and carry out specific functions. Therefore, if a family member is presenting a learning or behavior problem in the classroom, family efforts to cope with this problem become involved with an educational system that has established goals and procedures to which the family must respond and accommodate.

When applied to assessing family functioning, systems theory provides a framework for determining the areas in which the system is dysfunctional. The social worker focuses his/her attention on how power is distributed within a given family, how relationships are structured, how roles are defined, and how communication is used to convey messages. Using this framework in assessment enables the worker to identify those areas of family functioning that need to be strengthened and provide answers to these important questions. On the basis of an evaluation of the family as a system, the worker can determine the degree of dysfunctioning as well as the form that the dysfunctioning takes. The worker can, for example, observe difficulties in communication, identify the obstacles to effective communication and evaluate the significance of these communication problems in assessing the total family system. Or the worker may observe considerable confusion or conflict in role definitions in a given family system, resulting in a state of disorganization that threatens the family's solidarity.

A systems approach to assessment enables the worker to determine intervention goals designed to help the family resolve problems and overcome difficulties in functioning. The establishment of goals flows logically from conclusions reached in assessing the family systems. The assessment of the family power structure may indicate that changes in family structure are necessary. The goal is then formulated in specific terms. For example, if the assessment indicates a weak coalition between the parents, the goal of intervention is to strenghten their relationship. If the assessment indicates inadequate role performance, the goal is to enhance the ability of one or more family members to carry out their role functions. The process involves a further refinement of the goal in terms of specific changes expected to take place as a result of intervention. For example, the mother's inadequate role performance may be identified as an inability to cope with the child's temper tantrums. The goal is to help her develop effective ways of coping with the child's behavior. A husband and wife unsuccessful in resolving conflict are taught the skills needed to negotiate differences.

In the process of setting goals, the worker becomes aware of the necessity of setting priorities. In so doing, the worker takes into account several factors: (1) the feasibility of the goals; (2) the family's capacity to achieve the goals; (3) the obstacles in the social environment that may interfere with achieving the goals. Therefore, the worker consults with the family members in order to determine what goals are feasible and within the range of the family's capacity. Differences as to which goals have priority are also discussed and negotiated, and agreement is reached between the family and the social worker during the early stages of intervention. The contract between the worker and the family reflects their mutual agreement as to which goals will be pursued during the helping process.

The role of the worker relates to the assessment and the goals of intervention. In broad terms, the role of the worker is formulated with regard to what changes are to occur in one or more areas of family functioning, that is, the worker is an agent for change. In more specific terms, the worker acts as enabler, teacher, broker and advocate. All of these roles are often employed in working with any given family, but emphasis on one or two may be indicated in a certain situation, depending on the capacity of the family system to deal with problems and the nature of the difficulties to be resolved.

If the goal is to enhance role performance, the worker will serve as enabler and teacher. For example, the parent is expected to learn and apply sound child-management principles and techniques. The worker fulfills the role of teacher by providing information, modeling behavior, and establishing new forms of interaction between parent and child. If the goal is to find material resources, the worker takes the role of social broker, exploring the family's needs and eligibility for receiving assistance from appropriate community resources. Job training for a family member may be seen as a step toward the goal of making the family self-sufficient, in which case the role of the worker includes enabling the client to enroll in a program designed to accomplish this end. The system approach to assessment of family functioning leads the worker to a careful examination of the impact of the social environment on the family system. Making changes in the environment may be indicated as a goal of intervention. For example, changing the relationship between the child and the classroom teacher or between the child and his peers may be defined as a goal. In such cases, the social worker may take the role of mediator between the child and the teacher or peers in order to effect changes in the relationships. In some cases, the worker takes the role of advocate in order to protect the interests of one or more family members when unjust discrimination interferes with family functioning.

Role Theory

Understanding and using role theory are important in helping families resolve problems related to role functioning in the family system. The term, *role,* refers to socially prescribed behavior expected of a person who occupies a particular position in a social system (Perlman, 1968). In a family system, each member occupies a position defining his or her role as husband, wife, parent, or child. For the family system to function smoothly there must be agreement as to how these various roles are to be performed. There are certain expectations attached to certain roles. The father is expected to support his children. The mother is expected to care for the physical and emotional development of the children. The husband is expected to give affection and emotional support to his wife.

In some families, roles are defined in incongruent ways. Husbands and wives do not always have the same perception of what is required in their roles as marital partners. Nor do they always agree about their roles as parents. For example, the wife perceives her husband as the parent who enforces discipline on the children. The husband expects the wife to maintain high standards of orderliness in managing the household. Many marital disputes have their origin in differences in expectations of role performance. In assessing family functioning it is therefore important to explore how each member perceives his own role and how s/he perceives the role of other family members.

Problems in role functioning usually take the following forms: (1) conflict in role expectations; (2) inadequacy in role performance; (3) incapacity to carry out a social role. The role of the social worker differs according to the type of role dysfunctioning that is the area of concern. Conflict in role expectations requires that the worker take the role of teacher and mediator in order to help family members clarify their expectations and resolve differences in their perceptions of what each expects. Inadequacy in role performance often relates to the expectations that society attaches to a given role. Mothers who leave their children without supervision and fathers who do not provide for their families are designated as neglectful parents who are failing to meet the responsibilities attached to their social roles. Parents who abuse their children are failing to fulfill the role of protecting their children and providing a safe environment for them. The social worker takes the role of teacher and enabler in cases of inadequate role performance in almost any case. In cases of child neglect or abuse, the worker serves as an advocate for the child while also serving as the enabler whose goal is to improve the parents' role performance and provide a safe environment in the child's own home.

In some cases, the family member is concerned about his own inadequacies or deficiencies in a given role rather than in what others expect of him or her. In short, family members sometimes feel that they would like to function more adequately as marital partners or parents. The worker must assess this dissatisfaction to determine if, in fact, the mother is actually not a "good mother" by exploring her perception of what she expects of herself in this particular role. It is possible that her expectations exceed what she can reasonably do, in which case the worker's efforts are directed to changing her perception of her role performance. On the other hand, an exploration of how the mother functions in regard to some aspect of her role may indicate that change is desirable if not always essential. The client's view of desired changes in functioning vary widely. Some mothers indicate a need to improve their family's diet while others are more concerned about their inability to demonstrate affection. Opportunities for acquiring ability and skill in carrying out specific tasks are usually available through community resources. Classes in nutrition, child care, home and personal-income management are examples of resources for clients who wish to improve some special aspect of their family roles.

In assessing families where child abuse is involved, the worker gives special attention to the way in which family members carry out their roles. In such families the husband and wife, for example, each expect to not be responsible for their own behavior, including injury inflicted on their children. The parents expect the children to give them affection in any event, viewing children as sources of emotional gratification. As a consequence, children in abusing families are put in the position of fulfilling the role of parent, rather than child. Instead of the parents giving affection and support to the child, they expect the child to give them love and affection.

The worker's task in such cases is to help the family restructure relationships and redefine roles. The goal is to break symbiotic ties that are usually the crux of the problem. The partners are required to give one another affection. As they find gratification of their emotional needs through this improved marital relationship, the probability of child abuse is lessened. At the same time the worker enables the parents to carry out the tasks of being mother and father in new ways by providing information on normal child development. Once the parent understands that what s/he regards as "bad" behavior is actually normal behavior, the need for punishing the child unnecessarily is removed. In the role of teacher, the worker also demonstrates how nonviolent forms of child management can effectively control children; as parents learn new forms of discipline, there is less tendency to resort to harsh forms of punishment or to inflict injury on the child.

In working with disorganized, multiproblem families the goal takes the form of helping parents carry out their roles as leaders in the family system. In most cases, such parents fluctuate between overly controlling stages of "enmeshment" and stages of "disengagement" during which they pay little or no attention to their behavior (Minuchin, 1967). Parental inconsistency in making rules to limit children's behavior causes serious problems because the children have few clear and reasonable guides to follow. The task of the worker is to help the parents carry out their leadership role in the family by formulating their expectations of how the children are to behave in clear and reasonable terms and to be consistent in the enforcement of the standards they have set.

Communication Theory

Social workers and researchers who have observed family communication patterns come to interesting conclusions in regard to how messages are exchanged, the purposes that communication serves, and the effects of dysfunctional communication on individual family members. Some studies have led to the theory that mental disorders are brought on by continuous exposure to faulty communication processes producing psychotic systems in one of the family members (Bateson et al., 1956). In any case, there is general agreement that communication is an important component of the family system and plays a significant role in facilitating interaction among family members.

Communication involves more than the exchange of messages through words. Body language is an effective form of expression and often carries more meaning than a verbal message. Facial expression, body posture, tone of voice are all forms of communication. An affectionate embrace is often more to the point than words. Turning one's back on another person carries an unmistakable meaning. A clenched fist signals anger or tension. An outstretched hand says "Welcome."

Verbal communications are accompanied by nonverbal messages. In most cases, the nonverbal message is congruent with the verbal message. Body language reinforces or confirms what is spoken. However, such is not always the case. A simple statement, "I am fine," is sometimes accompanied by an expression of fatigue or pain. The intended message is, "I am hurting some, but I don't want you to worry about me." Or a wife sits apart from her husband, scowling at the television screen. He inquires if something is troubling her or if she is angry. She makes a denial saying, "Nothing's wrong," but at the same time begins to swing her leg vigorously and clasps her arms around her chest. These are obvious indications that the nonverbal message is the message that conveys the meaning actually intended.

Researchers who have observed family members attempt to carry out a task such as planning a picnic find that some families are able to communicate well and go about the matter efficiently. Other families engage in long irrelevant discussions and so are unable to make sense of what they are to accomplish. Eventually the process breaks down and the family is unable to complete the task. Trying to look into another's mind is another dysfunctional form of communication in which the receiver of the message makes an interpretation not intended by the person sending the message. Attempts to determine whether the message has been interpreted accurately is absent in dysfunctional patterns of communication. Failure to inquire into meanings leads to ambiguity and uncertainty.

In some families, the incongruity between verbal and nonverbal communication is subtle but pervasive. Moreover, family members are not free to inquire about the message and clarify the meaning that it was intended to convey. Consequently, both the sender and receiver are not sure they understand what is being said. If they respond to the verbal message, they are discounting the nonverbal message. This phenomenon has been called a "double-bind" because it is impossible to respond to contradictory messages. For example, the mother asks her young child to "come sit on mother's lap." The child smiles and moves toward the mother who then stiffens and pulls away. The child then hesitates to approach her. The mother sees the child's hesitation and remarks, "What's the matter? Don't you love me?" Consistent exposure to double-bind messages, say communication theorists, eventually causes the child to be totally confused and creates serious problems and barriers in developing clear communication (Jackson, 1960).

The term *mystification* has been used to describe how some families deal with conflict by befuddling, obscuring or masking what is happening. Masking does not *solve* the conflict, but it does conceal it. Family members use mystification to avoid facing conflict and to maintain the status quo. It is brought into play when a family member expresses feelings or ideas that threaten the family's solidarity. A child who complains about being unhappy is told that such a feeling is not possible. "You have no right to be that way. We have given you everything. How can you be so ungrateful?" The parents deny that what the child is saying actually exists. Through using mystification they can avoid facing and accepting the true state of affairs, but the child in turn comes to doubt the validity of her/his own perceptions (Laing, 1970).

Communication is used to define relationships among family members, and conveys messages as to who has a right to talk to whom and about what. The participants may define their relationships as *symmetrical* or *complementary*. If A boasts, B tries to top him. B then boasts even more and so the "one-upmanship" game continues in a symmetrical relationship. In complementary relationships, one person may be asssertive and the other submissive. Such relationships are based upon inequality. The male usually takes the dominant "one-up" position and the female assumes the submissive "one-down" position. Each partner behaves in a manner that will maintain this fit between them and they become locked into a fixed interaction pattern. Such communication patterns may reveal the relationship between sender and receiver. Struggles for a position of dominance and power are reflected in the messages that family members exchange (Haley, 1963).

In the course of the power struggle each member tries to redefine the relationship. Jockeying for control is found in all families. Most couples eventually find a suitable way to deal with these power struggles. In healthy families, the members constantly try to convey ideas and feelings clearly, honestly and openly. Family members are willing to listen to each other's points of view and everyone respects the need to share feelings. Rather than sending out double-bind or confusing messages, the family develops a capacity to convey meanings clearly and freely.

Healthy communication is essential to the resolution of conflict within the family system. Issues that threaten to divide the family can be brought into the open, discussed, and negotiated. *Negotiation* of conflict requires an ability to communicate effectively. The ability to state one's position clearly provides the basis for an exchange between bargaining partners. Negotiation of differences also involves the ability to listen and accurately interpret what is being said. If meanings are not clear, either party in the negotiation should ask for clarification until both are satisfied that they understand what is involved in solving the problem confronting them.

Because ineffectual communication is a principal source of difficulty in almost all families, social workers focus much attention on this area of family functioning. The first step in helping the family improve communication requires careful observation of family interaction during problem-solving. Such observations provide a basis for pinpointing how communication is used and where it fails. For example, if the therapist addresses the father and the mother responds while the father remains silent, the relationship between the partners is complementary. If the social worker observes that when the father makes a critical comment about the son, the mother calls attention to an irrelevant matter to avoid conflict, she is using mystification to prevent it.

When the worker sees a consistent pattern of communication, s/he can begin to call attention to family difficulties and suggest a different

approach to communicating feelings and ideas. The worker can
intervene by structuring the process in a manner that will require
family members to refrain from their habitual forms of interacting.
Communication exercises during the family session help the family
establish new communication pathways. For example, the worker
may request that the father and son talk to one another without the
participation of the mother in making a decision. The worker may
instruct the son to request something from the father, e.g. a bicycle,
a privilege, or money and observe how the father and son arrive at a
decision on the son's request. When difficulties arise, the worker can
"coach" the father or son by suggesting how they might change
their interaction and make it more effective.

The worker also serves as a model to the family. If s/he is careful to
communicate clearly and honestly, the family members can follow
the example. Several techniques can be used to help families communicate. The worker turns to a member of the family and asks for
clarification of what is meant by a given message. Phrases such as
"I am not sure that I understand what you mean" or "Could you tell
me a little bit more about how you feel" or "I think I may have
misunderstood you" are effective in showing the family how to check
meanings and indicate the importance the worker places on what
others say. The worker can also help the family to avoid sending
vague and ambiguous messages by inquiring into what is meant by
expressions such as "I wish he were more loving" or "I wish she
were more understanding." If family members can learn to make requests in specific behavioral terms, there is a greater possibility that
they can enter into effective negotiation. In short, the worker, as
model, takes on the role of enabler and teacher to help the family
improve communication skills.

Social Learning Theory

Social learning theory is based on the assumption that all behavior is
learned and that what we refer to as the individual's *personality* is the
sum total of learned behavior. People are products of their environment, behavior is the essence of personality. Therefore to understand
any person's problems in functioning, we must examine the environmental factors that shape behavior. This view of personality formation carries with it the tacit assumption that all behavior is malleable,
that behavior can either be extinguished or reinforced. The task of the
agent who involves the individual or family in therapy is to determine
which techniques are effective in diminishing objectionable behavior
and which are effective in increasing desired behavior.

The process of shaping, then, requires the selective use of some type of reinforcement. Once the reinforcer has been selected, the worker or another person in the immediate social environment (teacher or parent) applies the technique of rewarding acceptable or desired behavior. The kind and level of reinforcement is carefully controlled, given immediately and in the appropriate amount. Failing to reinforce is one way of diminishing objectionable behavior. Punishment is used to change behavior by withholding a positive reinforcer or applying an aversive stimulus (negative reinforcer).

Clinicians have recently extended the use of behavior modification to marital and family intervention. An increasing number of social workers have found it helpful in working with families as well as individuals. Objectionable behavior can be dealt with in and by the family, they point out. Before intervention is initiated, the worker makes an assessment that defines the behavior to be changed, the frequency with which it occurs, and the events that set it off. This assessment in behavioral terms becomes the basis for selecting an approach to bring about the desired change. The assessment usually includes information about what behavior is maladaptive in the identified patient and what changes each person would like to see in other family members. The worker also determines what environmental factors maintain the undesired behavior, with a view to effect change in the family to eliminate positive reinforcement of problematic behavior. For example, if the mother tries to comfort the child or control his temper outbursts by giving him food or affection, the child's tantrums are constantly being rewarded. The intervention plan would consider changes the mother should make to eliminate the behavior. In any case, the worker guides the family toward altering some reinforcement contingencies and developing new ones to reinforce acceptable behavior. The child will then be given attention when he displays adaptive behavior.

The implications of learning theory and behavior modification techniques for social work practice are numerous. The assessment process begins with defining the family problem in specific behavioral terms with goals related to effecting changes in specific behaviors. Therefore, the effectiveness of intervention can also be measured precisely and intervention techniques can be altered if the results prove disappointing.

Whether all family problems can be defined in terms of specific behavior remains somewhat dubious, but there are indications that it can be used effectively in helping families solve problems. The use of *operant-interpersonal therapy* to resolve marital problems is promising (Stuart, 1976). From the behavioral point of view, difficulties in the marital relationship can be resolved if the couple make contracts that reinforce changes in behavior. In successful marriages, the partners have reached a quid-pro-quo arrangement from which they both benefit. The wife agrees to go on a fishing trip with her husband if he will visit her parents the following weekend. The worker enables them to determine the terms of the contract and follows up to ascertain if the new arrangement is solving the problem. During the course of intervention, new problems can be dealt with by additional contracts. If the contract proves unsatisfactory, the partners can renegotiate and settle on mutually satisfying terms.

Teaching parents to use behavior modification techniques is effective when the family is having problems in child management. Abusing parents can be instructed how to use positive reinforcement as a method of controlling children's behavior and learn to substitute nonviolent behavior modifiers for corporal punishment. Disorganized families in which parents are in the stage of disengagement or enmeshment can learn behavioral techniques that will give them a sense of leadership and help them exercise their parental function more effectively. In short, social learning theory, when applied to families, helps parents help their children acquire and maintain certain behavior patterns. The worker's role is to outline the procedures for them and teach them how to carry them out to change behavior.

Social learning theory has also called attention to the influence of modeling on behavior. Models of social role are important in shaping the child's perception of what is "masculine" behavior and what is "feminine" behavior. Gender roles are defined within the family of origin by the mother and father. The growing child observes the interaction between his parents and learns what "marriage is all about" from his experiences within his own family. These experiences are carried over into his adult life because he models his own behavior on what he has observed. If his parents punished him excessively, beat and abused him, he will do the same to his own children, despite promises that "I'll never lay a hand on any kid of mine." Studies of conjugal violence show that modeling has a profound influence in producing wife beating. Violent behavior is learned and passed on from one generation to the next. The task of the social worker as an agent for change in preventing the use of violence to solve family problems is clear. We have learned from social learning theory that behavior can be changed and the cycle of violence can be broken.

**Table 8.1. *Summary of Concepts, Goals, and Social Worker
Roles Grouped by Major Theoretical Orientation.***

I. **Systems Theory**
  A. *Relevant Concepts*
    1. Family structure
    2. Homeostasis
    3. Scapegoating
    4. System input and output
  B. *Intervention Goals*
    1. Changing family structure
    2. Improving communication
    3. Restructuring relationships
    4. Changing the social
      environment
  C. *Social Worker Roles*
    1. Enabler
    2. Broker
    3. Advocate
    4. Teacher

II. **Role Theory**
  A. *Relevant Concepts*
    1. Role expectations
    2. Role performance
    3. Role incongruence
    4. Role conflict
  B. *Intervention Goals*
    1. Clarification of roles
    2. Accommodation to
      family roles
    3. Improvement in role
      performance
  C. *Social Worker Roles*
    1. Enabler
    2. Teacher
    3. Broker

III. **Communication Theory**
  A. *Relevant Concepts*
    1. Double-bind
    2. Mystification
    3. Complementary
      relationships
    4. Symmetrical
      relationships
  B. *Intervention Goals*
    1. Restructuring
      communication
    2. Negotiating
      conflicts
    3. Modifying
      relationships
  C. *Social Worker Roles*
    1. Teacher
    2. Enabler

IV. **Social Learning**
  A. *Relevant Concepts*
    1. Personality is behavior
    2. Behavior is learned
    3. Behavior is malleable
  B. *Intervention Goals*
    1. Changing individual
      behavior
    2. Changing marital
      interaction
    3. Changing family
      interaction
  C. *Social Worker Roles*
    1. Teacher
    2. Enabler

Combining and Integrating Approaches

Each approach to helping troubled families has some distinguishing characteristics, yet they all share the common purpose of enhancing the social functioning of the family unit and individual family members. The universal goal is to help families solve their problems effectively. Given this commitment to a common purpose social workers can consider several ways of achieving it. There is no *one* method of helping. Indeed, a combination of methods and techniques is often the most effective approach to solving family problems. Table 8.1 summarizes relevant concepts, goals of intervention and social worker roles in the four major theoretical orientations discussed: systems theory, role theory, communication theory and social learning theory.

The selection of a given approach to helping troubled families depends on the nature of the problem, the goal of intervention and the social worker's competence in using a certain model. Experience in the use of various helping approaches brings increased confidence in arriving at a decision about which will be most effective in working with a particular family. Many social workers find that a careful and skillful blending of models and techniques is useful and that an eclectic approach often provides the help that families need in solving problems.

*References*_____

Bateson, G., Jackson, D., Haley, J. & Weakland, J. Toward a theory of schizophrenia. *Behavior Science,* 1956, *1,* 251-264.

Haley, J. *Strategies of psychotherapy.* New York: Grune and Stratton, 1963.

Jackson, D. *The etiology of schizophrenia.* New York: Basic Books, 1960.

Laing, R. D., & Esterson, A. *Sanity, madness and the family.* Middlesex, England: Penquin, 1970.

Minuchin, S. et al. *Families of the slums.* New York: Basic Books, 1967.

Perlman, H. *Persona.* Chicago, University of Chicago Press: 1968.

Stuart, R. B. An operant interpersonal treatment for marital discord. In D. H. Olson (Ed.), *Treating relationships.* Lake Mills, Iowa: Graphic, 1976.

Index

A
Abused children
  approaches in helping, 140-152
  characteristics of, 139
  family planning and, 151
  foster care for, 144
  parents of, 137-139
  preschool for, 143
  punishment of, 139
Abusing parents
  assessment of, 141-142
  characteristics of, 138-140
  crisis intervention with, 149
  early identification of, 149
  goals of helping, 142
Ackerman, N., 5, 22, 39, 52, 63
Assessment
  factors in, 33-35
  family functioning, 174-175
  family interaction, 174
Attneave, C., 60, 63

B
Bagarozzi, D., 156, 172
Bateson, G., 39, 179, 186
Beavers, R., 24, 31, 39
Beck, D., 39, 99
Behavior modification
  intervention through, 183
  training in, 184
  modeling and, 184
Behavioral social work
  assessment in, 41, 44

changing parent-child interaction
  in, 42
changing marital interaction in,
  43, 45
mediator and, 42
modifying behavior through, 45
practice in, 156
seminars in, 156
techniques of, 156
training for, 155
Bell, J., 55, 63
Bowen, M., 53, 63

C
Carnegie Council on Children,
  92-95
Chaotic families, 31-32
Child abuse
  attitude toward, 140-141
  causes of, 133-140
  effects of, 132
  extent of, 132
  nature of, 131
  prevention of, 148-152
Child guidance, 170-171
Communication
  breakdown in, 20-21
  clarity in, 19
  conflict resolution and, 86
  dysfunctional, 19
  double bind in, 180
  family, 179

mystification in, 180
negotiation and, 86-87
problems in, 30
research in, 179
theory of, 179-182
Co-therapy, 164-165
Crisis intervention
    family crisis and, 47-48
    multiple impact therapy and, 49
    principles of, 46-47, 50
    purpose of, 50
    techniques of, 47

D

Divorce, 76-79
Disengagement, 106
Disorganized families, 101-109
    adolescent behavior in, 109
    coalitions in, 109
    health problems of, 105
    marital functioning in, 106-107
    overview of, 103-105
    parental functioning in, 106
    pathology in, 109-110
    social isolation in, 104
    socio-economic background of,
        103
    structure of, 105-107
Duhl, E., 161, 172

E

Enmeshment, 105
Environment
    health and, 90-91
    impact of, 90
    effecting changes in, 91-94
Epstein, L., 126, 129

F

Family advocacy
    effectiveness of, 98-99
    legal rights and, 96
    responsibility for, 97-98
    social worker's use of, 96-98
Family conflict
    competition and, 23
    control of, 21
    scapegoating and, 23
    sources of, 22
Family life cycle, 7-11
    marriage and, 8
    parenting stage in, 10
    patterns in, 11
    problems during, 10-11
Family relationships
    autonomous, 18
    changes in, 18-19
    sexual aspects of, 18
Family residential treatment, 144
Family sculpting, 161-162
Family structure, 24-27
    coalitions in, 24
    healthy, 28
    power base of, 24
    splits in, 24
Family systems
    abusing, 131-154
    dysfunctions in, 137-140
    healthy, 137-138
    violence in, 132-152
Family therapy
    changing relationships and, 84
    communication and, 53
    contracting in, 54
    defining problems in, 86
    diagnostic testing and, 160
    enhancing communication and,
        86

goals of, 51
negotiation of conflict in, 86
setting goals of, 83
structural, 54
supervision in, 161
training in, 159-161
Family violence, 132-152
assessment of, 141-142
causes of, 133-135
physical punishment and, 134, 139
prevention of, 148-153
social stress and, 135-136
Foster care, 144
Framo, J., 58, 63
Froelich, R., 163, 172

G
Gelles, R., 150, 153
Gil, D., 150, 153
Goal Attainment Scale, 142
Goals of intervention, 185-186
Group approaches
behavior rehearsal and, 57
group facilitators, 58
marital problem, 58
marital separation and, 76
parent training in, 57
stages in, 56
termination of, 56
Group therapy, 143
Guardian ad litem, 148
Gruenberg, P., 167, 172

H
Haley, J., 53, 63, 129, 165-167, 169, 170, 172, 181, 186
Hawkins, R., 63

Hollingshead, A., 14, 39
Hot lines, 143

I
Interpersonal Process Recall, 162, 163

J
Jackson, D., 180, 186
Justice, B., 142, 153
Justice, R., 142, 153

K
Kadushin, A., 111, 112, 129
Kagan, N., 162, 172
Keniston, K., 2, 5, 92, 99

L
Laing, D., 180, 186
Laquer, H., 58, 63
Lay therapy, 143
Lederer, W., 21, 23, 39
Lewis, J., 25, 26, 30, 39, 159, 172
Liberman, R., 54, 63

M
MacGregor, R., 49, 63
Manser, E., 95, 99
Martin, H., 133, 153
Marital functioning, 107
Marital problems
causes of, 66-68
negotiation and, 67-69
resolution of, 66-70
sexual functioning and, 69-70
Marital separations
adjustments to, 76-77
economic problems and, 75
effects of, 76-77
emotional reaction to, 74
group therapy and, 76-77
obsessive review and, 74

Minuchin, S., 54, 105-106, 125, 129, 178, 186
Multiple family therapy, 58-60
Multiproblem families
    advocacy for, 121
    community resources for, 120
    problem solving in, 122-125
    social worker roles in, 120-121
    task-centered casework with, 128

N
National Child Abuse Center, 133
Negotiation
    marital problems and, 66-67
    task performance and, 26
Network intervention
    application of, 62, 158-159
    goals in, 62
    seminars in, 157
    steps in, 60-61
    training for, 157
Neurosis, 33

P
Parent-child relations
    adolescent problems and, 78-79
    family therapy and, 79-82
    conflict in, 78-81
Parent education, 149-150
Parental functioning, 108-110
Perlman, H., 113, 129, 186
Personality adjustment
    disorders in, 87
    family therapy and, 87-90
    family structure and, 89-90
Poverty
    alleviation of, 91-93
    child abuse and, 151
    impact of, 91-93
    work incentives and, 92-93

Problem solving, 122-128
    communication and, 32, 125-126
    disorganized families and, 126
    effectiveness of, 126-128
    goals of, 113
    joint tasks in, 122-123
    negotiation and, 31
    purpose of, 112
    task centered approach in, 124
Protective services, 147-148
Punishment, 150-151

R
Reid, W., 126-127, 129
Relationships, 180
Role playing, 119, 163-165
Role theory, 176-179
Rosenbaum, M., 169, 172
Rueveni, U., 157, 172

S
Satir, V., 20, 39, 53, 63
Scherz, F., 20, 39
Schizophrenia, 33
Sexual problems, 69-73
    communication and, 71-72
    contract negotiation and, 72-73
Simulation, 119, 162-164
    family interview, 164
    family therapy, 163
    role playing and, 162-163
    training and, 162-165
Social environment, 11-15
    health services and, 13
    police protection and, 13-14
Social learning theory, 182-184
Social roles, 16-17, 177-179
    adaptation to, 16
    changes in, 16-17

conflict in, 16
Social services, 1
    access to, 93
    coordination of, 94
    family systems and, 93-95
Social stress
    child abuse and, 135-137, 151
    crisis and, 136
    poverty and, 135-137
Social systems
    effect on family, 14
    poverty and, 14
Social work
    behavioral, 155-157
    intervention through, 155
    preparation for, 155-172
    supervision in, 165-168
    training centers for, 170-171
Speck, R., 60, 63
Strauss, M., 133-135, 138, 153
Stuart, R., 184, 186
Supervision, 165-166
    clinical training through, 170
    family therapy, 165
    group, 165
    live, 169-170
    videotape recording in, 167
Systems theory, 173-179

T

Target problems, 116-120
Task-centered casework, 116-120
    analyzing obstacles in, 119
    developing strategies of, 118
    disorganized families and, 124
    effectiveness of, 127
    establishing incentives in, 118
    experiments in, 126-127
    planning tasks in, 117
    review of tasks in, 120
Thorman, G., 153

V

Videotape Recording
    supervision through, 168
    family therapy and, 169
    training in, 158-159
Voiland, A., 109, 129

W

Weiss, R., 74, 99
Wodarski, J., 156, 172
Wynne, L., 22, 30, 39

Y

Young, L., 104, 108, 110, 129

Z

Zuk, G., 54, 63